Oxford University Press
198 Madison Avenue, New York, NY 10016 USA
Great Clarendon Street, Oxford OX2 6DP England

Oxford New York
Athens Auckland Bangkok Bogotá Buenos Aires
Calcutta Cape Town Chennai Dar es Salaam Delhi
Florence Hong Kong Istanbul Karachi Kuala Lumpur
Madrid Melbourne Mexico City Mumbai Nairobi Paris
São Paolo Singapore Taipei Tokyo Toronto Warsaw

and associated companies in
Berlin Ibadan

OXFORD is a trademark of Oxford University Press

ISBN 0-19-435353-2

Copyright © 1999 Oxford University Press

Library of Congress Cataloging-in-Publication Data

Richards, Jack C.
    Springboard : student book 2 / Jack C. Richards
      p. Cm.
    ISBN 0-19-435353-2
    1. English language – – Textbooks for foreign speakers.
    2. English language – – Spoken English – – Problems,
    exercises, etc. 3. Listening – – Problems, exercises, etc.
    I. Title.
PE1128.R465 1997
428.3 ' 4 – – dc21   97-11076
                                                 CIP

No unauthorized photocopying

All rights reserved. No part of this publication may be reproduced, stored in a retrieval system, or transmitted, in any form or by any means, electronic, mechanical, photocopying, recording, or otherwise, without the prior written permission of Oxford University Press.

This book is sold subject to the condition that it shall not, by way of trade or otherwise, be lent, resold, hired out, or otherwise circulated without the publisher's prior consent in any form of binding or cover other than that in which it is published and without a similar condition including this condition being imposed on the subsequent purchaser.

Editorial Manager: Chris Foley
Developmental Editor: Karen Brock
Associate Editor: Paul MacIntyre
Editorial Assistant: Maura Tukey
Designer: Susan Brorein
Picture Researcher: Clare Maxwell
Production Manager: Abram Hall
Production and Prepress Services: PC&F, Inc.
Cover Design: Keithley and Associates Incorporated

Printing (last digit) 10 9 8 7 6 5 4 3 2 1

Printed in Hong Kong

Acknowledgments

Illustrations and realia by: Eliot Bergman, Scott MacNeill, Karen Minot, Rob Schuster, Jeff Seaver

Location and studio photography by: Rick Ashley

I Got You Babe by Sonny Bono
© 1965 (Renewed) Cotillion Music, Inc. & Chris Marc Music.
All Rights Administered by Warner-Tamerlane Publishing Corp.
All Rights Reserved. Used by Permission. Warner Bros. Publications U.S. Inc., Miami, FL 33014

p.16: Records from The Guinness Book of Records 1997 edn,
© 1996 Guinness Publishing Ltd. The Guinness Book of Records is a Trade Mark of Guinness Publishing Ltd.

p. 22: Illustration from THE TALE OF PETER RABBIT by Beatrix Potter © Frederick Warne & Co., 1902, 1987. Reproduced by kind permission of Frederick Warne & Co.

The publishers would like to thank the following for their permission to reproduce photographs: Michael Lipchitz/AP Photo; Hans Pfletchinger/Peter Arnold, Inc.; Rick Ashley; Bozell Worldwide, Inc.; Adamsmith, Ron Chapple, Travelpix/FPG International; Fujiko-Pro; Runk & Schoenberger/Grant Heilman; Dan Helms, Alan Becker, Michael Coyne, John P. Kelly, Yellow Dog Prod./The Image Bank; Alain Evrard, Universal Studios/Liaison International; NASA; Lester Glassner Collection/Neal Peters; Bob Allen, TR Youngstrom/Outside Images; Robert Brenner, Myrleen Ferguson/Photoedit; Jason James Richter, Universal Studios/Photofest; Bachmann, James King-Holmes/SPL/Photo Researchers; Ronnie Kaufman/The Stockmarket; Carlo Borlenghi/Stock Newport; Paul Chesley, Charles Mason, Joseph McBride, Jess Stock, Darryl Torckler, Art Wolfe/Tony Stone Images; Tony Stone Worldwide; Rob Van Petten; A.Ramey, Universal Studios, Mike Yamashita/Woodfin Camp, and Michael S. Yamashita.

The publishers would like to thank the following for permission to photograph their products: Givenchy, Inc.; Keenpac North Ltd; Nancy Stutman Calligraphics and Skyline Design; Nesnadny + Schwartz, Pyramid Books, and Setpoint/Unisource Paper Co.

There are instances where we have been unable to trace or contact the copyright holder before our printing deadline. We apologize for this apparent negligence. If notified, the publisher will be pleased to rectify any errors or omissions at the earliest opportunity.

Contents

Scope and Sequence — IV
Introduction — VI

UNIT

1	Money	2
2	Stress and Solutions	6
3	Friendship	10
4	Challenges	14
5	Globetrotters	18
6	Animals	22
7	Partners	26
8	Color and Design	30
9	Theme Parks	34
10	Values	38
11	Advertising	42
12	Mysteries and Beliefs	46

Project File — 50

PROJECT

1	Spending Diary	51
2	Stress Wheel	52
3	Rules of Friendship	53
4	Amazing Achievement	54
5	Exotic Getaway	55
6	Animal Mirror	56
7	Song Contest	57
8	T-Shirt Design	58
9	My Theme Park	59
10	Values Survey	60
11	Best Ad	61
12	Lucky For Me	62

Glossary — 63

Scope and Sequence

UNIT	TOPICS	SPEAKING ACTIVITIES	LISTENING ACTIVITIES	PROJECT
Unit 1 **Money** *Page 2*	• Spending Money • Where to Spend • Money Proverbs • Your Money Style	• Discussing spending habits • Talking about best places to buy • Exploring money proverbs • Survey of money styles	• Listening to items described • Recognizing attitudes	**Spending Diary** *Page 51*
Unit 2 **Stress and Solutions** *Page 6*	• Stressful Situations • Stress Meter • Stress Solutions • Stress Survey	• Talking about stressful situations • Ranking stressful situations • Giving examples of stress solutions • Survey of stress and solutions	• Identifying stressful situations • Listening for causes of stress and solutions	**Stress Wheel** *Page 52*
Unit 3 **Friendship** *Page 10*	• Best Friends • Best Friend Profile • The Test of Friendship • Friendly Advice	• Discussing friendship traits • Talking about a best friend • Answering questions about friendship • Giving advice to friends	• Recognizing friendship traits • Recognizing reasons and examples • Listening to magazine letters	**Rules of Friendship** *Page 53*
Unit 4 **Challenges** *Page 14*	• Challenging Sports • Sports Challenge • Fantastic Feats • Amazing Achievements	• Describing sports challenges • Evaluating sports • Reacting to feats • Planning a feat	• Identifying sports and listening for opinions • Identifying feats and listening for reasons	**Amazing Achievement** *Page 54*
Unit 5 **Globetrotters** *Page 18*	• Ready to Go • Smart Packers • Australian Getaway • Gold Coast Gems	• Describing vacations • Discussing vacation needs • Talking about an Australian vacation • Discussing Gold Coast activities	• Recognizing descriptions • Identifying activities	**Exotic Getaway** *Page 55*
Unit 6 **Animals** *Page 22*	• Animals Among Us • Favorite Characters • Animal Roles • Animal Rights Issues	• Talking about animals • Discussing favorite characters • Discussing animal roles • Survey of animal rights issues	• Recognizing descriptions • Recognizing opinions and reasons	**Animal Mirror** *Page 56*

iv

UNIT	TOPICS	SPEAKING ACTIVITIES	LISTENING ACTIVITIES	PROJECT
UNIT 7 **PARTNERS** *Page 26*	• Keys to a Successful Relationship • Terms of Endearment • Single or Married • Relationships	• Talking about relationship factors • Reacting to terms of endearment • Discussing being single and married • Survey about relationships	• Listening to and completing a song • Recognizing preferences	**SONG CONTEST** *Page 57*
UNIT 8 **COLOR AND DESIGN** *Page 30*	• The Meaning of Color • Find Your Color Temperature • Great T-shirts • Favorite Clothes	• Identifying and discussing colors • Talking about color favorites • Ranking by color and design • Survey of wardrobes	• Identifying items and preferences • Recognizing descriptions and preferences	**T-SHIRT DESIGN** *Page 58*
UNIT 9 **THEME PARKS** *Page 34*	• Theme Parks • The Best of the Parks • Culture World • Plan a Pavilion	• Talking about theme park activities • Survey of the best of the parks • Discussing Culture World attractions • Planning a pavilion	• Identifying places and predicting • Recognizing places and attitudes	**MY THEME PARK** *Page 59*
UNIT 10 **VALUES** *Page 38*	• Is It OK? • How Honest Are You? • Virtues • Wisdom From Others	• Discussing situations and conditions • Survey on honesty • Discussing virtues • Talking about learned values	• Recognizing speakers' choices and reasons • Listening for information and qualities	**VALUES SURVEY** *Page 60*
UNIT 11 **ADVERTISING** *Page 42*	• Logos • The Winning Bag • Great Magazine Ads • Advertising Survey	• Identifying and discussing design qualities • Choosing a winning design • Guessing ads and discussing effective ads • Survey of ads	• Identifying designs • Listening for qualities and descriptions	**BEST AD** *Page 61*
UNIT 12 **MYSTERIES AND BELIEFS** *Page 46*	• Nessie • World Mysteries • Personal Beliefs • Believe It or Not	• Discussing beliefs about Nessie • Discussing beliefs about world mysteries • Talking about personal beliefs • Survey on beliefs	• Listening to beliefs and explanations • Recognizing beliefs	**LUCKY FOR ME** *Page 62*

v

INTRODUCTION

Springboard Student Book 2 is the second in a two-level topic-based conversation and listening course for adult and young adult students at the pre-intermediate to intermediate level. It is organized around high-interest topics that encourage students to talk about what they are most interested in: their own lives, aspirations and interests.

Each topic in *Springboard* is explored from two perspectives and introduced by photographs or artwork that activate students' previous language knowledge and real-world experience. Short interactive tasks and personal surveys guide students toward conversational fluency and help them develop communication skills that can be put to immediate use in real-world situations. The listening component reinforces these skills as students develop listening strategies such as listening for gist, attitude and inference. A variety of international accents are a feature of the recorded dialogues so that students are exposed to English spoken as they may actually encounter it outside the classroom.

The topic-based syllabus of the book was shaped by the topics selected from student surveys. The principle underlying each unit is that students are motivated to talk about topics most closely connected to their lives. In addition, the language they need to discuss such topics should flow naturally from the topics themselves. For this reason, the language models, key expressions and vocabulary in *Springboard* are chosen for their usefulness in giving students clear guidance in developing conversational skills they need to discuss topics of importance to them.

The Project File further encourages students' personal involvement and responsibility for their own learning. This file of learner-centered projects provides students with the opportunity for creativity and personal expression as they interact to perform such projects as designing a T-shirt and planning a theme park. As students plan, carry out and share their projects with classmates, they are given the opportunity to bridge the gap between language study and language use.

UNIT STRUCTURE

Springboard contains 12 four-page units. Each unit is divided into 2 two-page lessons that are organized around a topic or theme. Each lesson opens with photographs or artwork which lead students into the topic of the lesson. Students are then given guided practice in the language and expressions they need to discuss each topic. A listening task provides further modeling and practice, and a culminating activity allows personalization of the topic through a communicative task. Each unit offers a variety of exercises and opportunities for pair and group work.

PROJECT FILE

The Project File follows unit twelve of *Springboard*. Twelve projects, one for each unit of the book, provide students with opportunities to extend the skills they have learned in each unit. Each project is accompanied with directions to students on how to plan, carry out and share their finished work with classmates. Suggestions for using projects to help students build a portfolio, a collection of completed work, is contained in the Teacher's Book. Additional suggestions for portfolio assessment, an evaluation of students' effort and work on the projects, is also contained in the Teacher's Book.

GLOSSARY

The *Springboard* Glossary, included in the back of the book, facilitates vocabulary development by including definitions in English of key vocabulary from the units. The concise definitions help focus students on learning vocabulary in context; therefore, definitions reflect the meaning of a word or phrase only as it is used in the units. A pronunciation key and examples of many of the words in context are also included. Photocopiable activities in the Teacher's Book provide further practice of the vocabulary in the Glossary and provide independent learning opportunities for students.

Teacher's Book

The *Springboard* Teacher's Book provides comprehensive suggestions for the most effective ways of presenting and exploiting the activities in the Student Book. In addition, a variety of options are often suggested with additional follow-up activities. The step-by-step notes provide both novice and experienced teachers practical guidance for classroom teaching. The Teacher's Book also offers suggestions for working with large and mixed ability classes and on how best to exploit the Project File and Glossary. Both levels of the *Springboard* Teacher's Books contain the following features:

- Step-by-step instructions for each activity
- Language, pronunciation, teaching and culture notes
- Photocopiable vocabulary development worksheets
- A photocopiable testing program
- Recommendations for assessment using project portfolios
- Photocopiable tapescripts for the audio program
- Answer keys to the Student Book

Thank you to the teachers, students and reviewers who provided valuable input in the development of *Springboard*:

Tricia Allan	Joanne Johnson	Sakae Onoda	Jason Sparks
Steve Cornwell	Josh Kurzweil	Mae-Ran Park	Alice Svendson
David Dykes	Hyun-Jung Kwon	Jack Perkins	Nolin Stratton
Jeff Fryckman	Brian Long	Carol Rinnert	Denise Swinnerton
Tim Grose	Kahoko Matsumoto	Stephen Ryan	Junko Yamanaka
Robert Hickling	Kristie Newgarden	Jennifer Sakano	Byunggon Yang
Weonsuk Hwang	Terry O'Brien	Ellen Shaw	

Finally, I would like to thank the publishing team at Oxford University Press— Karen Brock, Susan Brorein, Bev Curran, Chris Foley, Paul MacIntyre and Maura Tukey—who set the highest standards for ESL publishing and whose editorial suggestions and encouragement made the writing of this book a special pleasure. Special thanks also to the Oxford University Press staff in Japan, Korea and Taiwan.

Jack C. Richards
Auckland, New Zealand

UNIT 1 — MONEY

SPRINGBOARD

▶ SPENDING MONEY

A. Look at typical things people spend pocket money on. Complete the chart below with names of things you have spent money on recently.

	Clothing and Accessories	Books and Magazines	Entertainment	Odds and Ends
1.	_____	_____	_____	_____
2.	_____	_____	_____	_____
3.	_____	_____	_____	_____

B. PAIR WORK. How much money do you spend a month? Use your chart to talk about the things you spend money on.

A: So, how much do you spend a month on **clothing**?
B: *I guess I spend* about $50 or so.
A: Really? What kind of **clothing** do you usually spend money on?
B: *I probably spend* the most on...

Estimating

I guess
I suppose   *I spend...*
I'd say

I probably spend...

2 • UNIT 1 MONEY

LISTENING   CD 1: 2, 3

A. Listen to people talking about things they have bought recently. Number the pictures as you listen.

A. ☐   B. ☐   C. ☐   D. ☐

B. Listen again. What did the people do to get a good deal for their money? Check (✔) the correct boxes below.

	1.	2.	3.	4.
Compared Prices	☐	☐	☐	☐
Bargained	☐	☐	☐	☐
Bought it on Sale	☐	☐	☐	☐

WHERE TO SPEND

A. Where do you spend your money? Complete the **Best Places to Buy** chart below.

$ BEST PLACES TO BUY

fashionable shoes	a new pet	fun jewelry
CDs	foreign language books	Italian food
concert tickets	sports equipment	coffee and tea
electronic appliances	summer fashions	glasses or contact lenses

B. GROUP WORK. Use your charts to compare the best places to buy. Give reasons for your choices.

A: Where do you go for **fashionable shoes**?
B: Let's see. If I need **fashionable shoes, I go to...**
A: Why's that?
B: Oh, that's easy. They have the *greatest selection*.

If I need / When I need | fashionable shoes | I / I like to | go to...

Reasons
greatest | selection
largest | variety
 | latest | fashions
 | most stylish |
cheapest | prices
most reasonable |

UNIT 1 MONEY • 3

UNIT 1 MONEY

A. 1

B. 4

C. 5

D. 6

E. 2

F. 3

▶ MONEY PROVERBS

A. Match a proverb below with a picture.
1. The best things in life are free.
2. Save your pennies for a rainy day.
3. You can't take it with you when you go.
4. Time is money.
5. Money talks.
6. Money doesn't grow on trees.

B. PAIR WORK. Take turns explaining the proverbs in your own words. What other proverbs do you know?

	Guessing Meaning
A: *I think* **Money talks** *means* when you have money, people listen. What do you think? **B:** It could be. Or, *maybe it means* when you have money, you can get anything you want.	*I think it means...* *It means...* *It probably means...* *Maybe it means...*

C. GROUP WORK. Compare proverbs that describe your attitude to money.

> I like the proverb **Money talks.**
> If you have money, you can get anything you want.

4 • UNIT 1 MONEY

► LISTENING

A. Listen to Aki and Sam and then Sook and James talking about money. Write the number of the proverb that describes their attitude from the list of proverbs on page 4.

Name	Proverb	Attitude Similar To...		
1. Aki	_____	parents	friends	shoppers
Sam	_____	mother	father	brother
2. Sook	_____	friends	father	mother
James	_____	his family	another family	neighbor

B. Listen again and circle the people who influenced their attitude about money.

► YOUR MONEY STYLE

Complete the survey to determine your spending style. Then discuss your views.

$ MY MONEY STYLE

❶ If someone gave me $1000, I would
  - ⓐ spend it on myself.
  - ⓑ put it in the bank.
  - ⓒ buy something for my family.
  - ⓓ _____.

❷ I wish I could afford to buy (e.g., *a dog*, *some* shoes, *a lot of* jewelry) _____.

❸ The most I've ever spent on a gift is _____.

❹ If I needed to save money, I would try to stop spending money on _____(s).

❺ If I needed money to take a trip, I would
  - ⓐ ask my parents for it.
  - ⓑ borrow it from a friend.
  - ⓒ work part-time to save up for it.
  - ⓓ _____.

❻ If I needed to make some extra money, a good part-time job would be _____.

	Expressing Interest
A: If someone gave me $1000, I'd spend it on myself. B: *Is that right?* What would you buy? A: I'd love to buy a motorcycle. B: *I'm like you. I would* buy a...	*Is that right?* *That's nice.* *I'm like you. I would...* *I'm not like you. Instead, I would...*

UNIT 1 MONEY • 5

UNIT 2
SPRINGBOARD
STRESS AND SOLUTIONS

meeting a date's parents

going to the dentist

making a phone call in English

taking an exam

going for an interview

being a house guest

▶ STRESSFUL SITUATIONS

A. Which of the situations above are stressful for you? Mark an **S** in the boxes of situations you find stressful. Write two more situations you find stressful.

1. _____ 2. _____

B. PAIR WORK. Why are the situations above stressful? Use the model below to discuss possible reasons for each situation.

	Reasons
A: **Meeting a date's parents** is stressful for me. I'm afraid that *I'll say the wrong thing*. B: Yes, I find that stressful, too. OR Really? Not me. I don't find it stressful at all. A: How about you? What do you find stressful?	I'll — say the wrong thing. break something. get sick. feel a lot of pain. I'll make — a mistake. a fool of myself. I won't be able to answer a question.

6 • UNIT 2 STRESS AND SOLUTIONS

► LISTENING CD 1: 6, 7

A. Listen and check (✔) the situations Kate, Lee and Anne find stressful.

B. Listen again. Write the *reason* each person finds the situation stressful.

Name	Situation				Reason
	dancing	planes	taxis	dentist	
1. Kate					_____
2. Lee					_____
3. Anne					_____

► STRESS METER

A. How stressful are the situations below? Rank the situations from 1 (most stressful) to 8 (least stressful). Then plot the letters on the Stress Meter.

A. ___ Thinking about my future.
B. ___ Worrying about my weight.
C. ___ Worrying about an earthquake or other natural disasters.
D. ___ Having an argument with a friend.
E. ___ Having an argument with my parents.
F. ___ Getting caught in rush hour traffic.
G. ___ Giving a speech.
H. ___ Returning home alone at night.

B. GROUP WORK. Take turns talking about your stress meters.

A: What is the | most / least | stressful for you?
B: For me **thinking about my future** is the | most / least | stressful.
C: Really? Actually for me **having an argument with a friend** is the *most stressful* and **worrying about my weight** is the *least stressful*.

UNIT 2 STRESS AND SOLUTIONS • 7

UNIT 2 STRESS AND SOLUTIONS

▶ STRESS SOLUTIONS

A. PAIR WORK. Look at the photo of common stress solutions. Which of these work for you? Talk about them with your partner.

> A: Do you ever **have a massage** to help you relax?
> B: Yes, I do. It really helps. I feel great after a massage.
>   OR
>   No, I've never tried it.

B. GROUP WORK. What do you do to relieve stress in the following situations? Share your solutions.

1. You've had a busy day. Nothing went right. **You want to unwind.**
2. It's been raining for a week. **You want to escape from reality.**
3. You have an important exam coming up. **You want to relax.**

	Giving Examples
A: When **I want to unwind,** I take a hot bath. It really works for me. B: *What I do is...* C: *What works best for me is to...*	*What I do is...* *What works best for me is to...* *I find the best thing is to...* *You know what I do? I...*

8 • UNIT 2 STRESS AND SOLUTIONS

A.   B.   C.   D.

LISTENING   CD 1: 8, 9

A. Listen to people describing what they do when they want to unwind. Number the pictures from 1 to 4.

B. Listen again. Match Ken, Julia, Jim and Diana with the cause of stress they describe. Write the names below.

School	Home	Work	Shopping
1. _____	2. _____	3. _____	4. _____

STRESS SURVEY

A. What is stressful and what do you do? Write the cause of stress and a solution for each situation in the chart below.

SITUATION	YOU	STUDENT ONE	STUDENT TWO
School		Exams, sleep	
Home			
Work			
Shopping			

B. CLASS ACTIVITY. Ask two other students about their stress and solutions and fill in the chart. Use the model below.

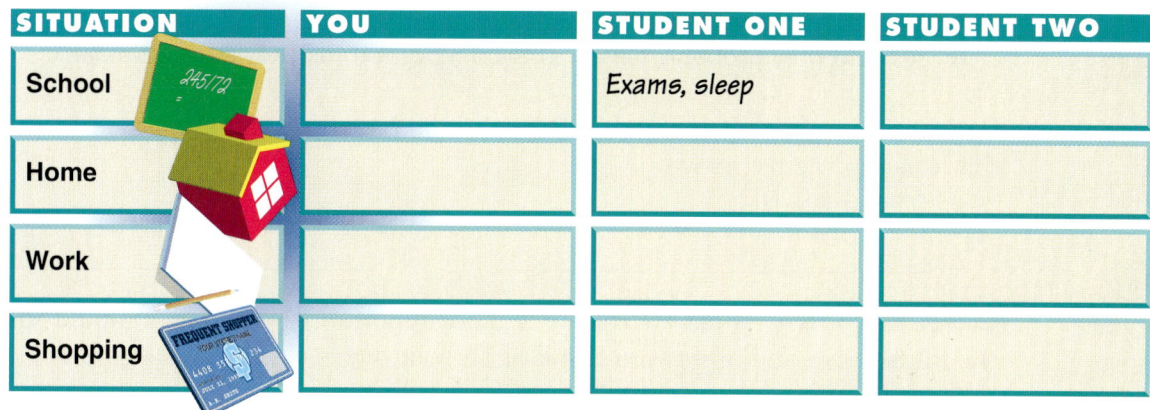

A: What is the most stressful thing at school and what's your solution?
B: At school? **Exams** are the most stressful, so I try to get a lot of **sleep** the night before.

UNIT 2 STRESS AND SOLUTIONS • 9

UNIT 3
SPRINGBOARD
FRIENDSHIP

Friendship Traits
sense of humor
personality
taste in music
fashion sense
opinions and beliefs

▸ BEST FRIENDS

A. PAIR WORK. Which traits do you think are similar for the two friends above? Give a reason for your guess.

> **A:** They probably *have a similar* **sense of humor.** They both like cartoons.
> **B:** Yes, and they probably *have a similar...* I don't think they *have a similar...*

B. List four traits that you and your best friend have in common. Use at least one trait that is *not* in the list above.

1. _____   3. _____
2. _____   4. _____

C. PAIR WORK. What are the three most important traits friends should share? Discuss the traits above and others you think of on your own.

> **A:** Do you think *friends need to have* a similar **sense of humor?**
> **B:** Yes, I think that's generally true, but not always. For example, my brother's friend...

Expressing Requirements

Friends need They have	to have...
They should They ought to	have...

10 • UNIT 3 FRIENDSHIP

A.

B.

C.

▶ LISTENING

A. Listen to Keiko, Jun and Kevin talking about their closest friends. Number the pictures as you listen.

B. Listen again. Check (✔) the *two* traits each pair of friends has in common.

	Sense of Humor	Personality	Taste in Music	Fashion Sense	Opinions and Beliefs
1. Keiko					
2. Jun					
3. Kevin					

▶ BEST FRIEND PROFILE

A. Complete the profile about your best friend.

✓ MY BEST FRIEND

① My best friend's name is _____.
② I met my best friend at _____.
③ My best friend and I have been friends for _____ years.
④ Two things we like to do together are _____.
⑤ Something that's different about us is _____.
⑥ Things we often talk about are _____.
⑦ Places we like to hang out are _____.
⑧ Three words that best describe my friend are _____, _____, and _____.

B. PAIR WORK. Take turns talking about your best friend. Ask your partner follow-up questions where appropriate.

	Follow-up Questions
A: My best friend's name is Young Kim. Two things we like to do together are go shopping and watch movies. B: Really? *Where do you* go shopping? A: Well, we usually go...	Where When *do you...?* How often Why

UNIT 3 FRIENDSHIP • 11

UNIT 3 FRIENDSHIP

A.

B.

C.

D.

▶ THE TEST OF FRIENDSHIP

A. People sometimes use the expressions below with friends. Match each expression with a picture.
1. I'd really like to but I can't.
2. Can you keep something a secret?
3. There's something I need to tell you.
4. Can you do me a favor?

B. Now match the expressions to the situations below. You may use an expression more than once.

a. ____ borrow money from a friend		d. ____ refuse to do something for a friend
b. ____ talk about a personal problem		e. ____ criticize a friend
c. ____ talk behind a friend's back		f. ____ share private information

C. PAIR WORK. What does it take to remain friends? Would you ever do the things in **B** above? Discuss each statement with your partner.

	Responding to Questions

A: Would you ever **borrow money from a friend?**
B: *Sure. Why not?*
    OR
    Not unless I really needed it.
A: *It depends.* I borrow money *only if* I forget my wallet.
	Sure. Why not?
	Possibly. For example...
	It depends.
	Not unless...
	Only if...
	I don't think so...

12 • UNIT 3 FRIENDSHIP

LISTENING

A. Listen to Naomi, Chet, Liza and Tom talking about why they broke off a close friendship. What qualities in the other person caused the problem? Match the person with a *reason*.

		Reasons	Example
1.	Naomi	never responded to the other person	_____
2.	Chet	lost her temper too easily	_____
3.	Liza	always wanted to be in control	_____
4.	Tom	never liked to share expenses	_____

B. Listen again. Write an *example* of something each person did that illustrates the quality.

FRIENDLY ADVICE

A. Listen and read the letters to a magazine below.

Ask Dr. Sue

Whenever I'm with a group of friends, I always get shy and am afraid I'll say something stupid. I'm worried they won't want to be friends anymore, so I usually don't talk at all. What should I do?
Shy in Singapore

I have this great friend and I really enjoy her company most of the time. But the problem is, she never listens to other people. And she talks about herself all of the time. I'm fed up. What should I do?
Sore Ears in Seoul

I think my best friend is taking me for granted lately. She spends all her time with her new boyfriend and only calls me when he's busy. Then she expects me to drop everything and do something with her. What should I do?
Ticked Off in Taipei

A guy I like a lot is great in many ways but he is really tight with money. He never offers to pay for anything and always forgets to pay back money he borrows. It really annoys me and my friends. What do you think is the best thing to do?
Tokyo Tightwad's Friend

B. GROUP WORK. What advice would you give to the people in these situations? Take turns giving advice.

A: What do you think **Shy in Singapore** should do?
B: First, *she shouldn't worry.*
C: Yes, and *maybe she should try to* relax and just be herself.
D: Well, *in this case the best thing to do is* ask people questions. People love to talk about themselves.

Giving Advice

| She
Maybe she
People like that | should(n't) | try to…
worry. |

In this case the best thing to do is…
One thing she could do is…

UNIT 3 FRIENDSHIP • 13

UNIT 4

CHALLENGES

SPRINGBOARD

A. kayaking

B. skydiving

C. snowboarding

D. rock climbing

E. scuba diving

F. yachting

▶ CHALLENGING SPORTS

A. PAIR WORK. What do you think of the sports above? Rank them from 1 (most exciting) to 6 (least exciting) and discuss your ranking with your partner.

A: For me the most exciting sport is **kayaking** because it's *risky*.
B: The most interesting for me is...
A: The second for me is **snowboarding**. I think **snowboarding** is *challenging*.

Adjectives to Describe Challenges

challenging	risky
different	rough
daring	frightening
thrilling	dangerous

B. GROUP WORK. Think of sports for the categories below and discuss them.

1. Sports you've tried and enjoyed.
2. Sports you've never tried but would like to.
3. Sports you've never tried and don't want to.

A: **Kayaking** is a sport I have tried a couple of times. I loved it. It was *different*, and I found it *challenging*.
B: A sport I'd love to try is **skydiving**. I love *thrilling* sports.
C: I'd hate it. It's too *dangerous* for me.

14 • UNIT 4 CHALLENGES

►LISTENING

A. Listen to people talking about sports they have taken part in. Number the pictures from 1 to 4.

A.

B.

C.

D.

B. Listen again and check (✔) the best word to describe each person's opinion of the sport.

1. ☐ great	2. ☐ challenging	3. ☐ dangerous	4. ☐ exciting
☐ dangerous	☐ fun	☐ thrilling	☐ frightening

►SPORTS CHALLENGE

GROUP WORK. Fill in the sports chart below. Then discuss your choices.

⚪ THE WIDE WORLD OF SPORTS

① a rough sport

② an exciting indoor sport

③ a challenging non-team sport

④ a good sport for older people

⑤ an unusual sport from another country

⑥ a thrilling sport that involves animals

⑦ an exciting racquet sport

⑧ a good rainy day sport

	Expressing Choices
A: What do you think is **a rough sport**? B: *For me* **a rough sport** *is...* because it's *dangerous* and it's... C: *Another really* **rough** *one is...*	*For me* | **a rough sport** *is...* *I think* *Another really* **rough** *one is...* *...is also very* **rough**.

UNIT 4 CHALLENGES • 15

UNIT 4　CHALLENGES

▶ Fantastic Feats

A. PAIR WORK. Look at the records for fantastic feats above. Which do you think is the most impressive? Which is the least impressive? Why?

> A: I think the most impressive record is the **oyster opening** one. That's *absolutely incredible*.
> B: I like the **kissing** record best. That's *really cool*.
> A: What's the least impressive one for you?

Reactions	
absolutely incredible	pretty pointless
pretty amazing	totally ridiculous
really something / really cool	just plain dumb

B. PAIR WORK. Why do you think people try to set new records? Add another reason, then rank the reasons from 1 (most popular) to 6 (least popular).

____ to become famous　　　　____ to do something no one has done before

____ to make money　　　　　____ to make themselves feel good

____ to achieve a personal goal　____ to _____

> A: I think the most important reason is they want *to...*
> B: Maybe it's also because they are trying *to...*
> A: Another factor is that they want *to...*

LISTENING

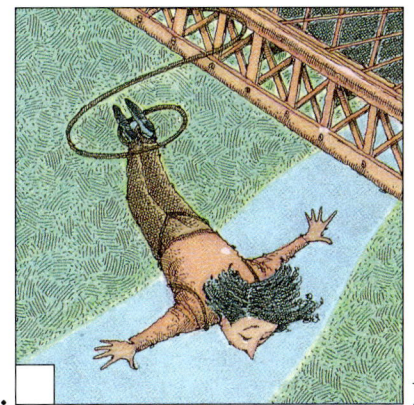
A.

B.

C.

D.

E.

F.

A. Listen to people talking about feats they have accomplished and number the pictures from 1 to 6.

B. Listen again. Write the *feat* each person achieved and the *reason* each performed it.

Feat	Reason		Feat	Reason
1.		4.		
2.		5.		
3.		6.		

AMAZING ACHIEVEMENTS

A. GROUP WORK. Plan a record-breaking feat for each of the types of feats below.
1. Eating or Drinking
2. Sports or Games

	Suggestions
A: For the **eating feat**, what about having someone... B: Maybe. And the winner would be the one who... C: Or *how about getting people to try to...*	What about having someone... How about getting people to try to... How about an event where someone has to... What about an event where you have to...

B. CLASS ACTIVITY. Present your group's record-breaking feat to the class. Vote for the best feat in each category.

Our feat is a(n) **eating feat**. Someone has to eat...

UNIT 4 CHALLENGES • 17

UNIT 5 — GLOBETROTTERS

SPRINGBOARD

▶ READY TO GO

A. PAIR WORK. What kind of a trip would you be planning with bags packed like the ones above? Choose adjectives to describe each one.

> **A:** With this one, you'd be planning an *action-packed* vacation and one that's...
> **B:** You would probably be planning on going to...
> **A:** And you'd probably...

Describing Vacations	
action-packed	adventuresome
fast-paced	laid-back
a thrill a minute	get away from it all
carefree	calm

B. PAIR WORK. What kind of vacation would you prefer? What would you plan on doing on your vacation?

> **A:** I'd prefer a *fast-paced, action-packed* vacation. I'd plan on seeing and doing as much as I could.
> **B:** Really? Not me. I'd prefer a *carefree* vacation. You know, like lying in the sun at the beach every day.

C. What are the five most important things you'd pack for your vacation?

LISTENING

A. Listen to people packing for a trip. Where do you think each person is going? Number the photos from 1 to 4.

B. Listen again. Write two items each person will pack.

A. _____ B. _____ C. _____ D. _____

SMART PACKERS

A. Choose one of the trips above. Write three necessary items you would pack in your suitcase for the categories below.

CLOTHING AND ACCESSORIES	COSMETICS AND HEALTH ITEMS	OTHER

B. GROUP WORK. Find other students who chose the same trip as you. Then decide on the three most important items to bring on your trip.

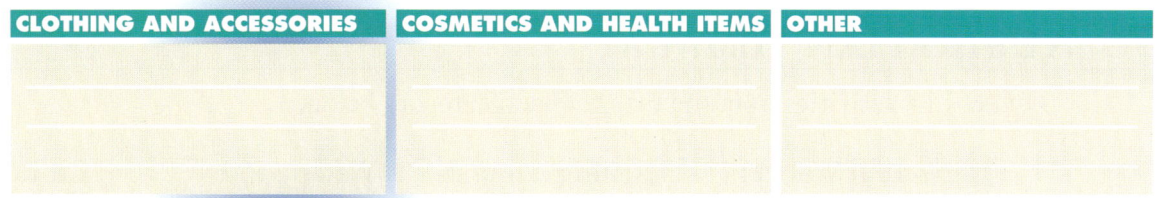

A: For a **Parisian holiday,** *we'd probably need...* and *we should probably take...*
B: And *it would be a good idea to take...*
A: *Would we need...?*

Anticipating

We'd probably need...
We should probably take...
It would be a good idea to take...

Would we need...?
How about taking...?
What else do you think we'd need...?

UNIT 5 GLOBETROTTERS • 19

UNIT 5 **GLOBETROTTERS**

▶ **AUSTRALIAN GETAWAY**

A. List activities from the map for each category below.

1. Natural Wonders	2. Exciting Animals	3. Water Sports	4. Cultural Fun
_____	_____	_____	_____
_____	_____	_____	_____

B. **PAIR WORK.** Which activities look most interesting to you? Discuss items from the map and others you may know.

> A: What are some things you would want to do on an Australian getaway?
> B: Let's see. I'd like a chance to **pet kangaroos, have a night at the opera** and **see Ayers Rock**.
> A: Yeah, I'd like to **pet kangaroos**, but I'd also really like to **cuddle a koala** and **visit the Outback**.

LISTENING

Listen to a travel agent describing an adventure tour in Queensland, Australia. Number a picture for each day described.

QUEENSLAND ADVENTURE TOUR

Day___   Day___   Day___   Day___   Day___   Day___

GOLD COAST GEMS

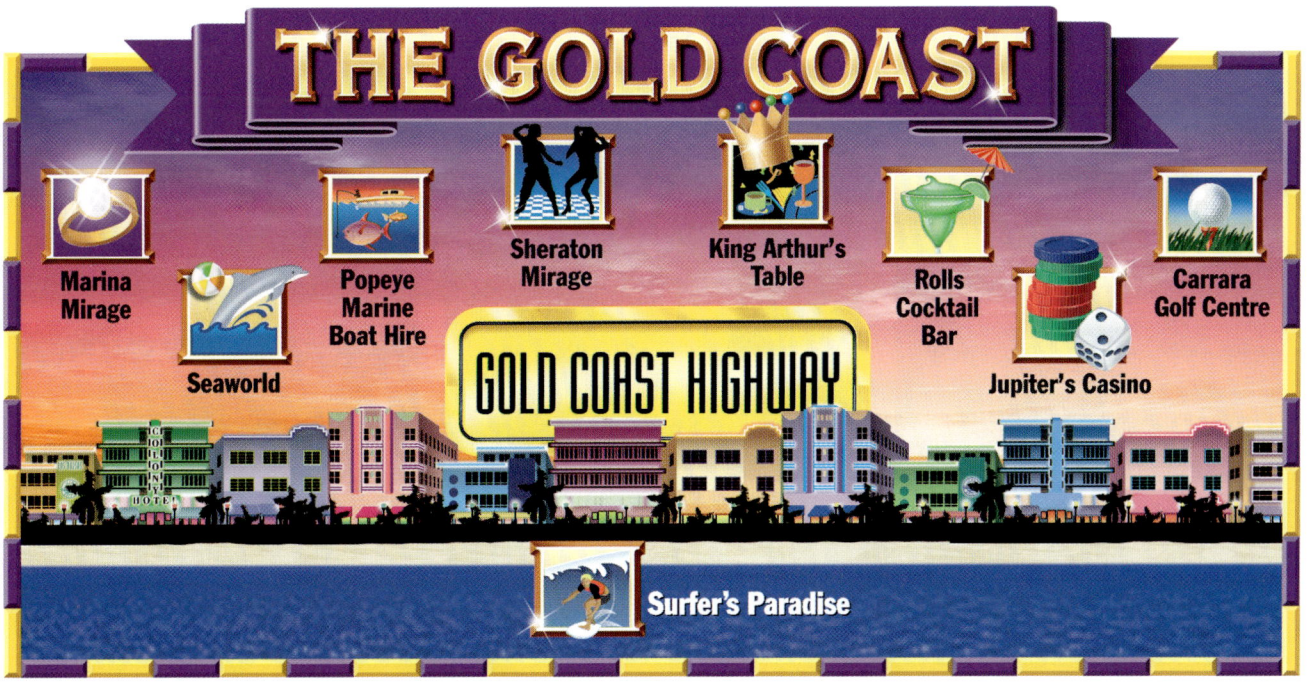

A. PAIR WORK. Where are the hot spots on the Gold Coast? Look at the map and decide where you could do the activities below.

1. sip an exotic drink
2. practice teeing off
3. bite into a juicy steak
4. gamble all night long
5. pet dolphins
6. dance your heart out
7. buy opal jewelry
8. catch a grouper
9. get a great tan

> A: Where could you go to **sip an exotic drink**?
> B: You could sip an exotic drink at **Rolls cocktail bar** or the **Sheraton Mirage disco**.
> A: Yeah, **Rolls cocktail bar** sounds interesting to me.

B. GROUP WORK. What are the top three things to do on the Gold Coast for your group? Share your group's top three with the class.

> If we went to the Gold Coast, we'd **gamble all night long at Jupiter's Casino,** we'd...

UNIT 5 Globetrotters • 21

UNIT 6

ANIMALS

SPRINGBOARD

Godzilla

Doraemon

Peter Rabbit

Jaws

Babe

Keiko

▶ ANIMALS AMONG US

A. PAIR WORK. Look at the photos of famous animals. Discuss your reaction to them with your partner.

	Adjectives to Describe Animals	
	+	**–**
A: What do you think of **Godzilla**?	adorable	ugly
B: I think he's *ugly*, and he's also a little *scary*.	cute	horrible
	cuddly	scary
A: What about **Keiko**?	friendly	creepy
B: She looks..., but she's also very...	smart	disgusting

B. PAIR WORK. What are *four* other animals you can describe with words from the box?

A: I think spiders are *disgusting*.
B: *Disgusting*? Why?
A: I hate their legs, and their heads are *ugly*. Yuk!

22 • UNIT 6 ANIMALS

▶ LISTENING

A. Listen to people talking about their pets. Number the pet talked about in each conversation.

B. Listen again. Write the *problem* each pet has.

1. _____   4. _____
2. _____   5. _____
3. _____   6. _____

▶ FAVORITE CHARACTERS

A. Complete the chart below with your favorite animal characters.

★ FAVORITE ANIMAL CHARACTERS

	NAME OF ANIMAL	KIND OF ANIMAL	TITLE OF WORK	DESCRIBING WORD
Movie or TV Show	Chance	dog	Homeward Bound	playful
Animation				
Comic Book				
Storybook				

B. GROUP WORK. Take turns discussing your favorites from the chart. Then report your group's choices to the class.

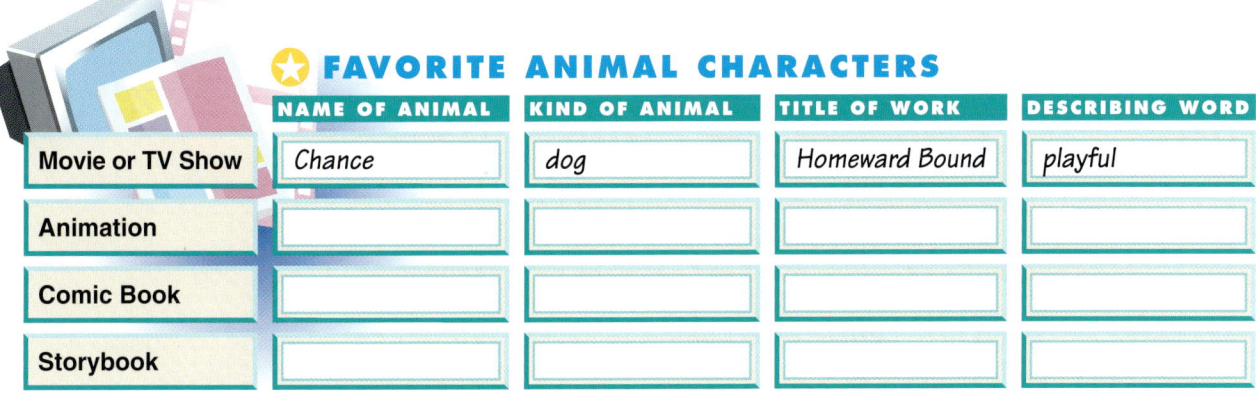

A: I like *Chance*, the *dog* from the **movie** *Homeward Bound*, because he is *playful*.
B: My favorite is...
C: Hey, me too. How about for a **comic book**? My favorite is...

UNIT 6 ANIMALS • 23

UNIT 6 ANIMALS

A

B

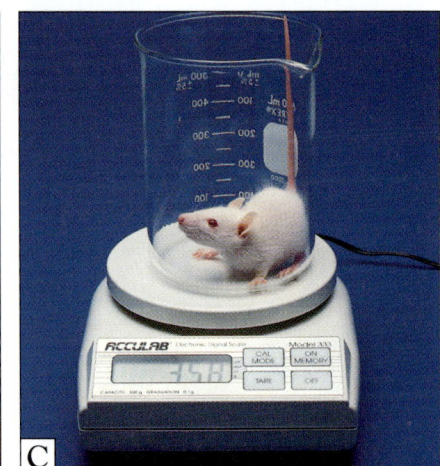
C

D

E

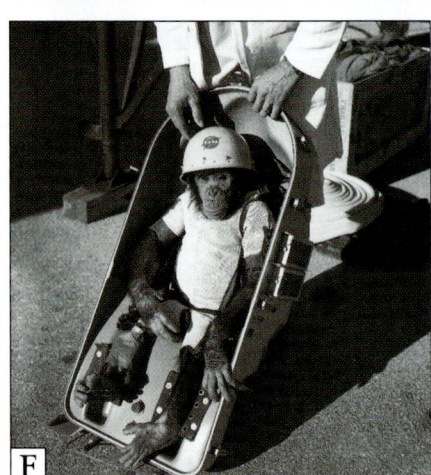
F

▶ ANIMAL ROLES

A. PAIR WORK. Look at some of the ways that animals and humans interact. List animals from above or others you know for the items below.

1. trusted companion _____
2. worker _____
3. organ donor _____
4. space traveler _____
5. feared enemy _____
6. entertainer _____
7. scientific participant _____
8. protector _____

> A: Well, a dog is often a **trusted companion**.
> B: Yes, and a cat can be too. But I guess the most common would be a dog.

B. PAIR WORK. What do you and your partner think of the animal roles above? Discuss at least *three* roles.

	Vocabulary to Describe Opinions		
A: I think it's *good* for an animal to be a **trusted companion**.	good	not so bad	cruel
B: Me too. And I think it's *OK* for an animal to be a(n)...	fair	OK	unfair
	necessary	not a problem	wrong
A: Really? I don't think it's *fair*...	educational		uncivilized
	natural		unnatural

24 • UNIT 6 ANIMALS

► LISTENING

A. Listen to Koji, Kana, Phil and Hideko discussing the use of animals in research. Check (✔) *for* or *against* for each person.

B. Listen again. Match each person with a *reason*.

	For	Against	Reason
1. Koji	☐	☐	_____ a. not necessary to use animals
2. Kana	☐	☐	_____ b. animals are for us to use
3. Phil	☐	☐	_____ c. better than using humans
4. Hideko	☐	☐	_____ d. causes suffering for animals

► ANIMAL RIGHTS ISSUES

A. Read the survey about animal rights below. Check (✔) the statements you agree with OR add statements of your own.

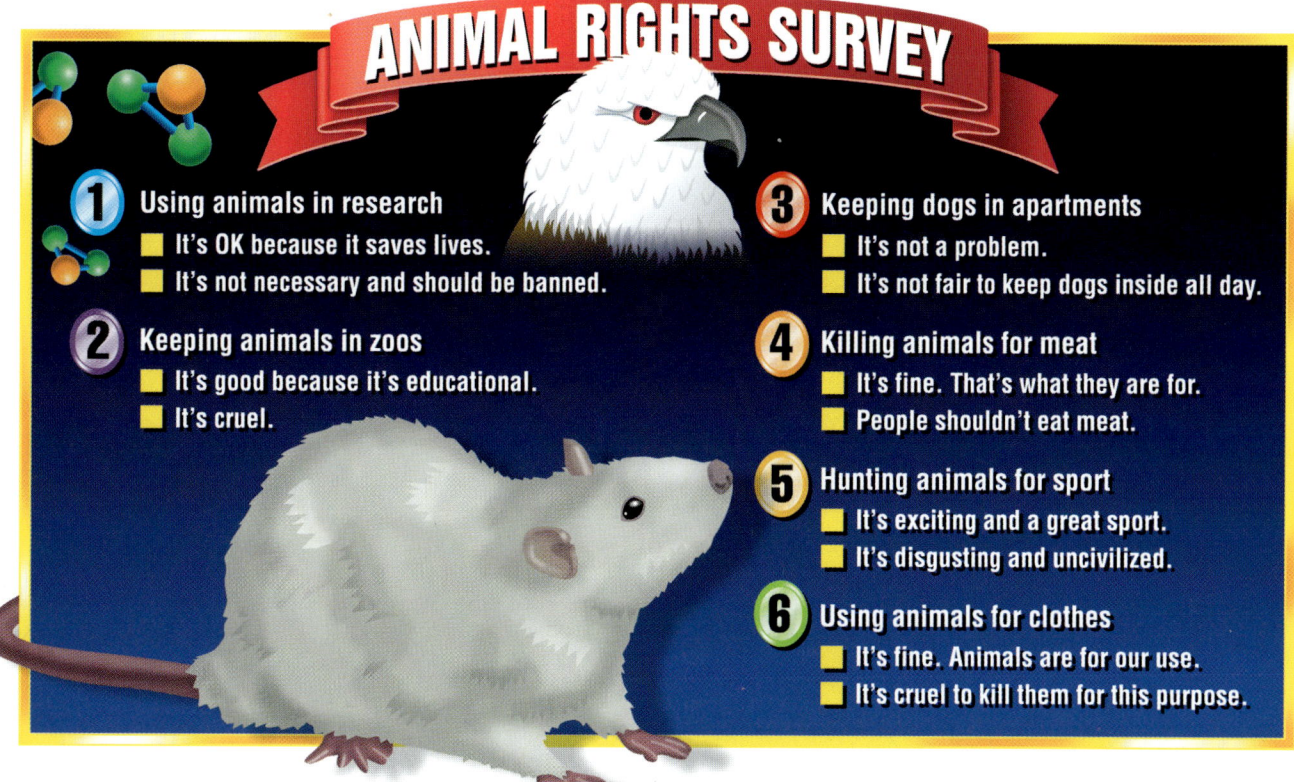

ANIMAL RIGHTS SURVEY

1. **Using animals in research**
   ☐ It's OK because it saves lives.
   ☐ It's not necessary and should be banned.

2. **Keeping animals in zoos**
   ☐ It's good because it's educational.
   ☐ It's cruel.

3. **Keeping dogs in apartments**
   ☐ It's not a problem.
   ☐ It's not fair to keep dogs inside all day.

4. **Killing animals for meat**
   ☐ It's fine. That's what they are for.
   ☐ People shouldn't eat meat.

5. **Hunting animals for sport**
   ☐ It's exciting and a great sport.
   ☐ It's disgusting and uncivilized.

6. **Using animals for clothes**
   ☐ It's fine. Animals are for our use.
   ☐ It's cruel to kill them for this purpose.

B. GROUP WORK. Discuss these issues in your group. Then share your discussion with the class.

A: How do you feel about **using animals in research?** **B:** Personally, I feel... **C:** As far as I'm concerned...	**Expressing Opinions** *Personally, I feel...* *As far as I'm concerned...* *I feel strongly that...*

As far as **using animals in research**	we think most of us feel most feel strongly	that...

UNIT 6 ANIMALS • 25

UNIT 7 PARTNERS

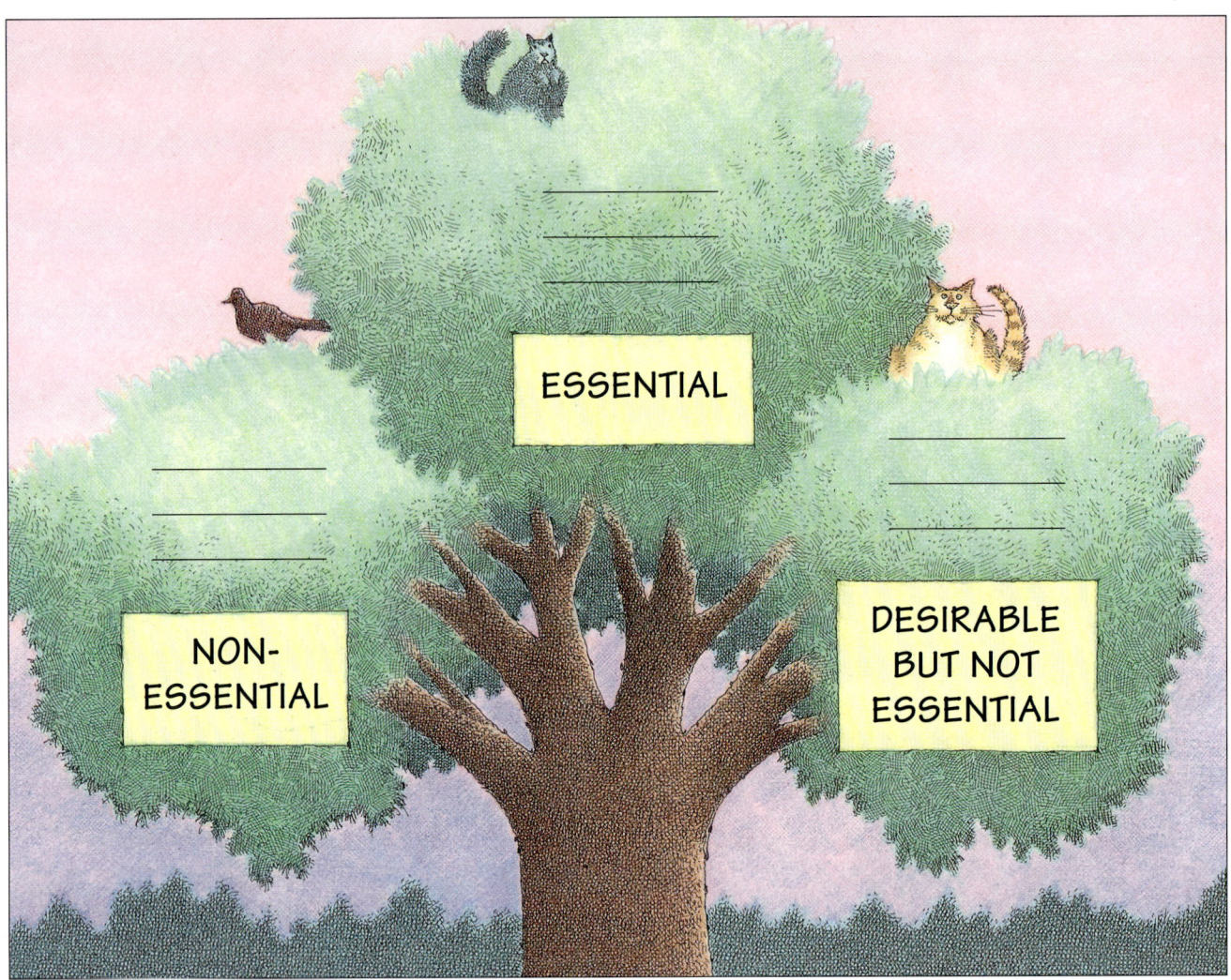

▶ KEYS TO A SUCCESSFUL RELATIONSHIP

A. How important do you think the factors below are in a relationship? Write the number of each factor on the diagram where you think it belongs.

1. looks
2. personality
3. intelligence
4. interests
5. age
6. career goals
7. sense of humor
8. family background
9. financial situation

B. PAIR WORK. Talk about your diagram with your partner.

	Expressing Importance
A: How important do you think **looks** are? OR **personality** is?	It's important. / essential.
	It matters a lot.
B: For me they are / it is important.	It's fairly important. / something to consider. / insignificant.
A: Is **personality** important to you?	
B: Yes, it matters a lot.	It doesn't matter very much.

26 • UNIT 7 PARTNERS

I Got You Babe

A. Listen to the classic song about partners, *I Got You Babe*.

B. **PAIR WORK.** Listen again. Complete the song with numbers from the word list.

They say we're young and we don't _____,
Won't find out till we _____.
Well, I don't know why that's _____
'Cause you got me, baby I got _____.

Babe,
I got _____, babe,
I got you, babe,

They say our love won't pay the _____,
Before it's earned, our money's always _____.
I guess that's so, we don't have a _____,
But at least I'm sure of all the things we _____.

Refrain

I got flowers in the _____.
I got you, you wear my _____,
And when I'm sad, you're a _____,
And if I get scared, you're always _____.

And then they say your hair's too _____,
But I don't care, with you I can't do _____.
Then put your warm little hand in _____,
There ain't no hill or mountain we can't _____.

Refrain

I got you to hold my hand.
I got you to understand.
I got you to walk with me.
I got you to talk to me.
I got you to kiss goodnight.
I got you to hold me tight.
I got you, I won't let go.
I got you who loves me so.
I got you babe.

1. Spring 2. rent 3. long 4. know 5. mine 6. pot 7. true 8. clown 9. you
10. ring 11. got 12. around 13. spent 14. wrong 15. grow 16. climb 17. you

C. **CLASS ACTIVITY.** Now sing the song.

Terms of Endearment

A. **PAIR WORK.** Look at some common terms of endearment English speakers sometimes use with partners. Talk about how they sound to you.

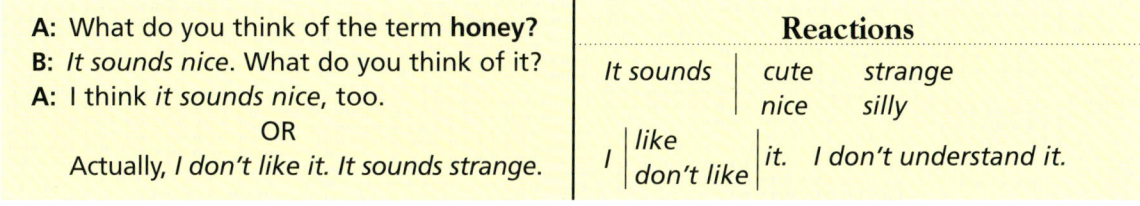

B. Share your favorite term of endearment in your language with your partner.

UNIT 7 PARTNERS • 27

UNIT 7 PARTNERS

A.

B.

C.

D.

E.

F.

▶ SINGLE OR MARRIED

A. Match statements single and married people have said with the pictures above.

1. You've always got someone to share your thoughts with.
2. You have someone to grow old with.
3. You aren't tied down to the same person.
4. There's a chance for a family life.
5. You're free to come home whenever you like.
6. You can spend your time and money however you wish.

B. PAIR WORK. What do you think are reasons people give for *staying single* or *getting married*? Choose items from the box and others of your own.

	Reasons	
	Staying Single	**Getting Married**
A: I think a reason for **staying single** is they *like their independence*. B: Really? I think they *are too busy with a career*. A: Another reason is they...	like their independence are too busy with a career can't find the right person don't want the responsibility	want to raise a family feel pressured by their family have found the love of their life want the security

28 • UNIT 7 PARTNERS

► LISTENING CD 2: 5, 6

A. Listen to Yuko, Simon, Lisa, Bryan, and Alex discussing their preferences for *single* or *married* life. Check which they prefer.

B. Listen again. Write one *reason* for each person's preference.

	Preference Single	Preference Married	Reason
1. Yuko	☐	☐	_____
2. Simon	☐	☐	_____
3. Lisa	☐	☐	_____
4. Bryan	☐	☐	_____
5. Alex	☐	☐	_____

► RELATIONSHIPS

GROUP WORK. Complete the survey below about relationships. Then discuss your views on relationships.

♡ RELATIONSHIP SURVEY

	Strongly agree	Somewhat disagree	Strongly disagree
❶ It is important to get your parents' approval of a marriage partner.	☐	☐	☐
❷ Everyone should marry before the age of 25.	☐	☐	☐
❸ Partners treat each other as equals.	☐	☐	☐
❹ It is OK to have more than one boyfriend or girlfriend at the same time.	☐	☐	☐
❺ Arranged marriages end up happier than love marriages.	☐	☐	☐
❻ Divorce is never OK.	☐	☐	☐
❼ Looks, personality and intelligence are equally important.	☐	☐	☐
❽ Sense of humor in a partner is more important than his financial situation.	☐	☐	☐
❾ Having the same beliefs and opinions makes a relationship boring.	☐	☐	☐
❿ Couples with the same cultural background have fewer problems.	☐	☐	☐

A: Do you agree that **it's important to get your parents' approval of a marriage partner?**
B: Yes, I **strongly agree** with that. *I believe that* if your parents don't approve, it will cause a problem between you and your parents.
C: Not me. I **strongly disagree**. *As far as I'm concerned...*

Expressing Beliefs

I believe / I feel that...

As far as I'm concerned...

In my opinion... / experience...

UNIT 8

SPRINGBOARD

COLOR AND DESIGN

cobalt blue
fire engine red
kelly green
lavender
lemon yellow
lime green
magenta
periwinkle blue
tangerine
turquoise blue

▶ THE MEANING OF COLOR

A. PAIR WORK. How many of the colors in the list can you find in the picture? Take turns identifying the colors.

> I think this is... .
> This is probably... .
> This might be... .

B. PAIR WORK. Take turns answering the question "What are two colors that...?" for each of the items below.
1. go well together?
2. don't go well together or clash?
3. create a warm feeling?
4. strike you as cold and unfriendly?
5. are bold and dramatic?
6. you would never wear?
7. you would like in your room?
8. you like best?

A: What are two colors that go well together? B: I think **lavender** and **cobalt blue** go well together. A: *Well, yes maybe.* I think **magenta** and **turquoise blue** go well together too.	**Responding to an Opinion** *Definitely.* *I agree.* *Well, yes maybe.* *Do you think so?* *I'm not sure about that.*

30 • UNIT 8 COLOR AND DESIGN

LISTENING CD 2: 7, 8

A.

B.

C.

D.

E.

F.

A. Listen to Amy and Sam talking about the items above. Number the item they discuss in each conversation.

B. Listen again. Would they like to have the item described? Check (✔) *would like* or *wouldn't like* below.

	1.	2.	3.	4.	5.	6.
Would Like	☐	☐	☐	☐	☐	☐
Wouldn't Like	☐	☐	☐	☐	☐	☐

FIND YOUR COLOR TEMPERATURE

GROUP WORK. Take turns talking about colors.

COLOR SURVEY

1 What is your favorite color?

My favorite color is _____.

2 What colors best express your personality?

_____ and _____ best express my personality.

3 What colors express these moods and feelings for you: passion, anger, peace, sadness, spirituality?

For me, _____ expresses _____.
         (color)

4 Are there any colors you don't like to wear? Why?

I don't like to wear _____ because _____.

5 What colors do you think go well in a a) bedroom b) kitchen c) living room?

_____ and _____ go well in a _____.
 (color)   (color)

6 Would you like to change the color(s) of the room you are in now? How?

No, I wouldn't. **or** Yes, I would. I'd like to change the color(s) of the room to _____ and _____.

UNIT 8 COLOR AND DESIGN

UNIT 8 COLOR AND DESIGN

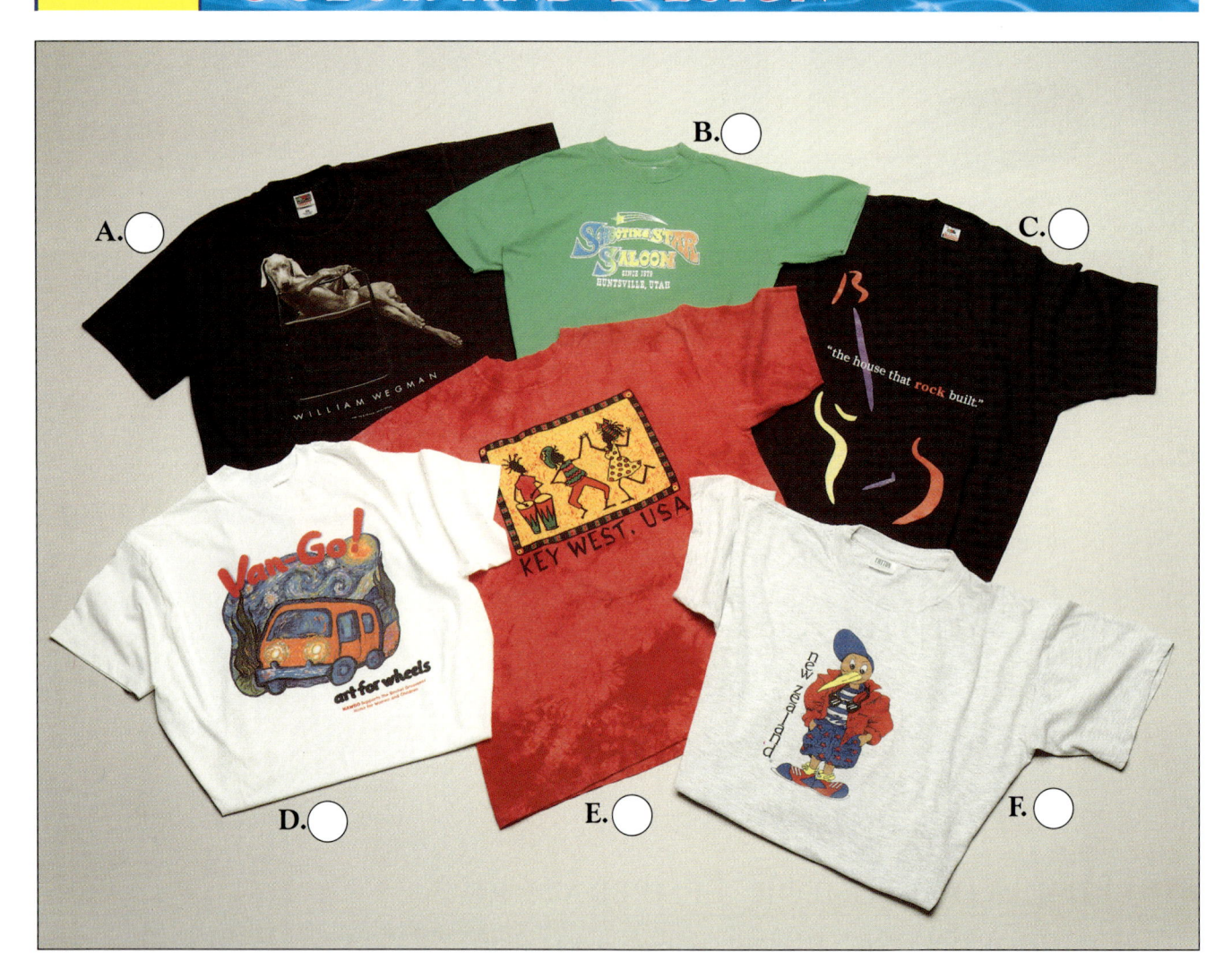

GREAT T-SHIRTS

A. PAIR WORK. What do you think of the T-shirts in the picture? Rank them from 1(best design) to 6. Give reasons for your ranking.

	Adjectives to Describe Colors and Design	
A: I like **A** the best. The design is / colors are appealing. B: I prefer **B**. It's...	appealing interesting striking cool	drab boring not very original ugly

B. GROUP WORK. What is your favorite T-shirt to wear? Discuss what it looks like and why you like it.

A: I've got a great T-shirt from Hawaii. The colors are *cool* and the design is *interesting*. It's got a beach and waves on it.
B: Mine is a plain white T-shirt with nothing on it. It's *not very original*, but simple is best.
C: My favorite T-shirt is *cool*. It's full of holes.

► LISTENING

A. Listen to people describing others at a party. Number the person described in each conversation.

B. Listen again. Write what the speakers *like* or *dislike* most about what each person is wearing.

1. _____
2. _____
3. _____
4. _____
5. _____
6. _____

► FAVORITE CLOTHES

A. Fill in the chart below with items you own.

❓ MY CLOTHES WARDROBE

DO YOU HAVE SOMETHING...?	
with striking colors	
with a unique design	
with holes	
comfortable but doesn't look great	
up-to-date	
you received as a gift and don't like	

B. GROUP WORK. Take turns describing items.

> A: I've got a great swimsuit **with striking colors**. It's black, gold and magenta. I love it.
> B: My favorite is a skirt I got in Mexico. It's orange and kelly green with...
> C: My cobalt blue and lavender T-shirt **doesn't look great,** but is **comfortable** to wear.

UNIT 8 COLOR AND DESIGN • 33

UNIT 9

SPRINGBOARD

THEME PARKS

Water World
- speed down a giant water slide
- swim in wave pools
- ride in a submarine

Dinosaur World
- enjoy a multimedia dinosaur show
- walk through a tropical landscape
- take an unforgettable river ride

Movie World
- go behind the screens into movies
- see the latest special effects
- buy studio souvenirs

Future World
- see the latest computer-controlled shows
- meet aliens
- ride to the moon

▶ THEME PARKS

A. PAIR WORK. Look at the different theme parks above. Talk about some of the things you would like to do at the parks.

> A: At **Water World** I'd love to **speed down a giant water slide**.
> B: Yeah, me too. **Swimming in wave pools** sounds fun too.
> A: How about at **Dinosaur World**?

B. PAIR WORK. What are your favorite kinds of things to do at theme parks? Choose activities from the box and others of your own.

> A: What's your favorite thing to do at a theme park?
> B: My favorite thing to do is to *go on rides*.
> A: I like that too. OR Not me.

Activities
go on rides	watch other people
visit the gift shops	take lots of pictures
eat lots of different foods	see a show

LISTENING

Listen to people at Dinosaur World. In the picture above number the place described in each conversation.

THE BEST OF THE PARKS

A. Complete the **Best of the Parks** survey.

✓ BEST OF THE PARKS

① In the last two years I have been to a theme park or amusement park _____ times.
② My favorite park is _____.
③ The scariest ride I've been on is _____.
④ My advice for anyone going to a theme park is _____.
⑤ The best souvenir I've ever bought is _____.
⑥ The most romantic ride I have ever been on is _____.
⑦ The park with the best value for money is _____.
⑧ The most fun show to watch is _____.

B. GROUP WORK. Take turns asking group members about their survey.

A: *How many times* have you been to a theme (or amusement) park in the last two years?
B: Let's see. I'd say about 20.
C: 20? Wow! *What's your favorite* park?
B: Oh, that's easy. It's...

Questions

How many times...?

What's | your favorite...? | the most romantic...?
| the scariest...? | the park with the best...?
| your advice...? | the most fun...?
| the best souvenir...?

UNIT 9 THEME PARKS • 35

UNIT 9   **THEME PARKS**

[Map of Culture World showing:]

- **ANCIENT CHINA**: treasures of the Imperial Palace, Beijing Opera, Great Wall exhibit
- **INDONESIAN WONDERLAND**: temple sound and light show, traditional dances, craft fair
- **USA TODAY**: space exhibit, movie museum, Rock 'n' Roll Hall of Fame
- **ROMANTIC ITALY**: Colosseum, Italian food fair, gondola ride
- **SURPRISING NEW ZEALAND**: Maori Art exhibit, farm show, kiwi birds

CULTURE WORLD — Welcome!

▶ CULTURE WORLD

A. PAIR WORK. Look at the map of Culture World. Where do you think you can probably do the following things?

	Attraction Activities
A: Where do you think you can *tour ancient ruins*? B: You could do that at **Ancient China** at the **Great Wall exhibit**. A: Yes, and I guess you could at **Romantic Italy** too. You could see the **Colosseum**.	tour ancient ruins see models of famous Hollywood stars milk a cow have a thrilling experience hear some unusual music see two-thousand-year-old vases and dishes see wood carvers at work see what the inside of a satellite looks like

B. PAIR WORK. Share your favorite attraction at each area of Culture World with your partner.

My favorite attraction at **Indonesian Wonderland** would be the **temple sound and light show**. At **Ancient China** it would be the **Beijing Opera**...

LISTENING

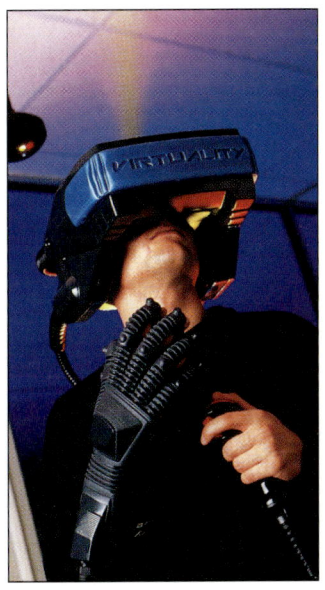

CD 2: 12, 13

A. _____   B. _____   C. _____   D. _____

A. Listen to Don, Emi, Amanda and Michael reacting to some of the things they have just seen at Culture World. Number the pictures from 1 to 4.

B. Listen again. How do you think each person rated each place? Check (✓) *really cool*, *not bad* or *save it for next time* for each person.

	1. Don	2. Emi	3. Amanda	4. Michael
*** really cool	☐	☐	☐	☐
** not bad	☐	☐	☐	☐
* save it for next time	☐	☐	☐	☐

PLAN A PAVILION

A. PAIR WORK. Plan a pavilion for Culture World. Choose a culture you know well (it can be your own). Suggest two interesting things for visitors to do and see for the categories below.

Traditional Culture	Art and Architecture	Science and Industry
_____	_____	_____
_____	_____	_____

A: *Maybe* for **traditional culture** *we could have* an exhibit of old costumes.
B: Sure, or *how about having* a folk dancing display with dances from all the different regions?

Suggestions
Maybe we could have...
Why don't we have...?
How about having...?

B. GROUP WORK. Present your ideas in groups.

A: We thought we would have one exhibit of old costumes. It would have...
B: We are also going to have a folk dancing display.

UNIT 9 THEME PARKS • 37

UNIT 10

VALUES

SPRINGBOARD

A.
B.
C.
D.
E.
F.

▶ Is It OK?

A. PAIR WORK. What do you think the people above are thinking? Match each statement with a picture.

1. I've always wanted one like this.
2. This must be a letter about his job.
3. I wonder who he's calling at midnight.
4. No one would mind if I ate just one.
5. My friend won't mind helping me.
6. The dog ate my paper. Really!

B. PAIR WORK. How serious do you think the situations below are? Add one more of your own, then rank the list below from 1 (most serious) to 8 (least serious). Discuss them with your partner.

_____ break a promise to your parents
_____ lie about something
_____ cheat on a test
_____ read someone else's mail
_____ tell a secret you promised to keep
_____ take something from a hotel or restaurant
_____ listen in on someone's private phone call
_____ _____

A: Would you ever **break a promise to your parents**?
B: Well, not usually, but maybe *I might if* I had a really good reason.
A: Me too.

Expressing Conditions
I might if...
Maybe I would if...
I would only if...
I would never...

38 • UNIT 10 VALUES

LISTENING

A. Listen to William and Maya discussing promises, lies and secrets. Check (✔) if they *agree* or *disagree* with each other.

B. Listen again. When is it OK for William and Maya to do these things? Write *N* for Never or *D* for It Depends in the chart.

	Agree	Disagree	When Is It OK? William	Maya
1. You should never break a promise.	☐	☐	_____	_____
2. You should never tell a lie.	☐	☐	_____	_____
3. You should never tell a secret.	☐	☐	_____	_____

How Honest Are You?

GROUP WORK. Answer the questions. Then score the survey and discuss them in a group.

HONESTY SURVEY

Yes | No | Maybe

1. You find a wallet on the street with lots and lots of money in it. *Do you take some of the money?*
2. You just love the towels in your hotel. *Do you put one in your bag when you leave?*
3. You buy five items at a store. The clerk only charges you for four. *Do you keep the fifth item?*
4. You lose your expensive watch at the beach. Your insurance will only pay for it if it's stolen. *Do you report it stolen?*
5. Your boyfriend/girlfriend is on a trip abroad. *Do you telephone him or her from work to save money?*
6. You are surfing the Internet. You find the perfect story for your homework assignment. *Do you copy it and not tell your teacher?*
7. You find a bootleg copy of your favorite CD at a flea market. *Do you buy it?*
8. You forgot about a big exam and didn't study. Your best friend studied hard and is very smart. *Do you sit near him during the exam?*
9. Someone you know sells tickets at a movie theater. He can let you in for free. *Do you accept his offer?*

Scoring:
Give 2 points for each NO,
1 point for each MAYBE,
and no points for each YES.
Add up your score.

18	You are very honest.
12-17	You are pretty honest most of the time.
7-11	You could be more honest.
1-6	Carry on like this and you could get into trouble.
0	You would make a great politician or business person.

A: What did you put for number 1?
B: I put **No** for this one. I don't think it's right to keep the money, even if it belongs to someone who is very rich.
A: I put **Maybe.** If I really needed the money, perhaps I'd keep it.

UNIT 10 VALUES • 39

UNIT 10 VALUES

A. Generosity — "It is better to give than to receive."

B. Self-Sacrifice — "I'd give you the shirt off my back."

C. Perseverance — "I never give up."

D. Modesty — "I didn't do much really."

E. Honesty — "I think this belongs to you."

F. Ambition — "For me, the sky's the limit."

G. Loyalty — "I'm a friend to the end."

▶ VIRTUES

A. PAIR WORK. Look at the newspaper headlines below. Which virtues do the news makers possess? Match a quality from above with a headline.

1. ☐ Taxi driver rewarded $2,000 for returning $20,000
2. ☐ Swimmer, 70, crosses English Channel in 5th try
3. ☐ Restaurant owner rewards long-serving staff member with $25,000 car
4. ☐ Donor gives $3 million to children's hospital
5. ☐ Dog enters burning building to wake sleeping owner

B. PAIR WORK. Share your responses in **A** with your partner.

A: This shows **loyalty**.
B: And it also shows **perseverance**.
A: What about **generosity**?
B: No, I don't think so. This headline shows **generosity**, I think.

40 • UNIT 10 VALUES

LISTENING

A. Listen to the news stories and write *who* and *what* the story is about in the chart.

B. Listen again and write down *two* qualities you think each story illustrates.

Story	Who	What	Quality
1.			_____ _____
2.			_____ _____
3.			_____ _____
4.			_____ _____

WISDOM FROM OTHERS

Words of Wisdom

Our lives are like a candle in the wind.
— C. Sandburg

The only way to have a friend is to be one.
— Emerson

Isn't it a great pleasure to learn and relearn again?
— Confucius

GROUP WORK. Whom do you think people learn these values from? Check (✔) a response for each value. Then compare with group members. Can you give an example from your life?

♥ LEARNED VALUES

VALUE	LEARN BY YOURSELF	FROM YOUR FAMILY	FROM SOMEONE ELSE
Honesty	☐	☐	☐
Generosity	☐	☐	☐
Loyalty	☐	☐	☐

A: I believe you learn **honesty** mainly from your parents.
B: But you can also learn it from your friends and from the people you hang around with. In my own case, I think the person who taught me **honesty** was...

UNIT 11 ADVERTISING

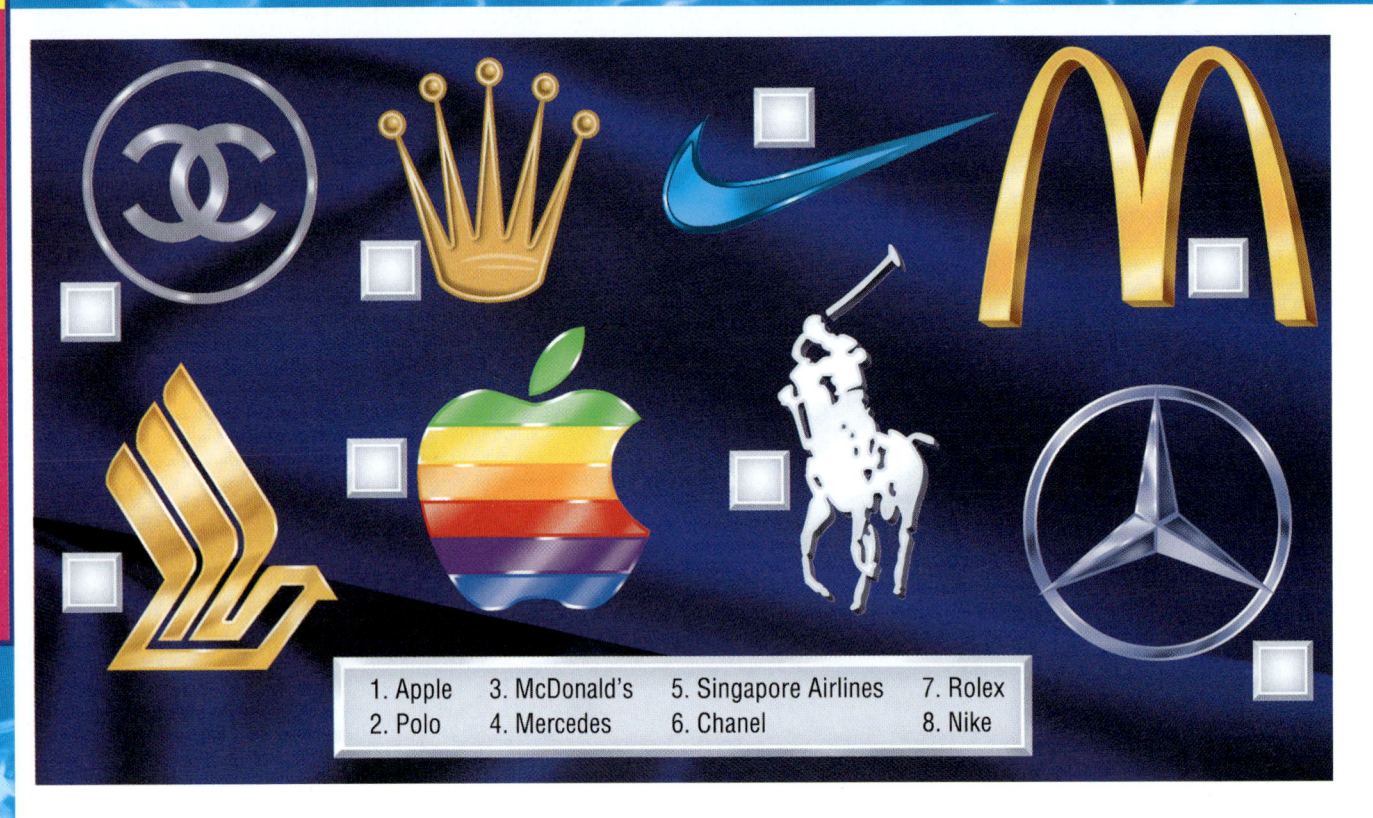

SPRINGBOARD

1. Apple	3. McDonald's	5. Singapore Airlines	7. Rolex
2. Polo	4. Mercedes	6. Chanel	8. Nike

▶ LOGOS

A. Match the logos above with a company name from the logo list.

B. PAIR WORK. Which logos are the most effective? Discuss the design qualities of the logos with your partner.

	Design Qualities	
A: I think the **Apple** logo *is* very *effective*. It *has bold colors* and *a clever design*.	has: bold colors / good graphics	a: clever design / classy look
B: How about the **Polo** logo? I think it *is effective*. It's *eye-catching* too.	is: effective / easy to remember / simple	eye-catching / unusual / creative
A: Yeah. And this one *is eye-catching* too.		

C. GROUP WORK. How many other logos can you remember? Choose the best logo you know for the items below and discuss them.

	Best Logo
1. Car	
2. Clothing or accessories	
3. Sports team	
4. Fast-food chain	

Rolex has the best logo for jewelry because it is *simple* and *easy to remember*.

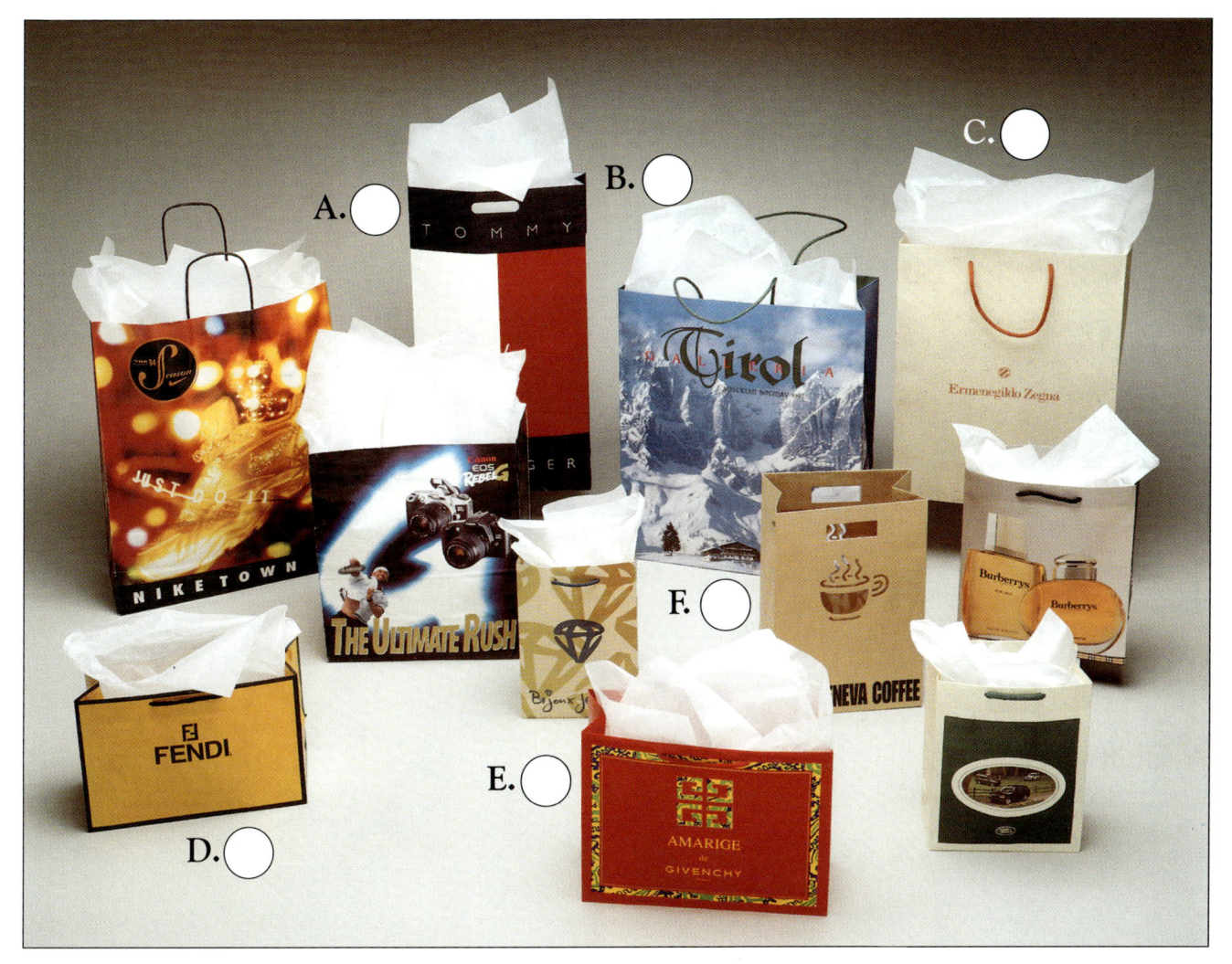

►LISTENING   CD 2: 18, 19

A. Listen to a designer discussing the shopping bags above. Number the bags as you listen.

B. Listen again. Write at least one *design quality* the speaker mentions for each bag.

Design Qualities	
1. _____	4. _____
2. _____	5. _____
3. _____	6. _____

►THE WINNING BAG

A. GROUP WORK. Which shopping bag should win the design contest? As a group, choose the winning bag. Be sure to use the **Design Qualities** on page 42.

B. Present your choice to the class and explain why you chose it.

> A: We like **A** best because we think it's *creative* and *easy to remember*. Also, we think...
> B: **D** is not very *eye-catching* and it doesn't have...
> C: **B** is OK, but not as good as the others because...

UNIT 11 ADVERTISING • 43

UNIT 11 ADVERTISING

A

B

C

D

▶ GREAT MAGAZINE ADS

A. PAIR WORK. Can you guess what the ads above are for? Talk about possibilities with your partner.

	Expressing Probability and Possibility	
A: What do you think this is an ad for? B: *It must be* an ad for… C: Yes, *it looks like*…	It | must be… looks like… probably is…	I | guess… suppose this is… wonder if…

B. What makes an effective magazine ad? Add one more to the list below. Then check (✓) the three most important to you.

____ causes you to think   ____ uses appealing people   ____ looks very dramatic
____ uses good photography   ____ looks distinctive or unusual   ____ _____

C. GROUP WORK. Discuss your views on what makes an effective magazine ad.

One of the most important factors is that it **causes you**…
Another important thing is that it **uses**…
I think whether it **looks distinctive** is less important.

44 • UNIT 11 ADVERTISING

LISTENING

A. Listen to people discussing effective TV ads. What quality do they like most in each ad? Check (✔) one item for each conversation.

B. Listen again. Write the *product advertised* for each conversation.

	Qualities		Product Advertised
1. ☐ good actor	☐ clever photography	☐ great music	_____
2. ☐ great humor	☐ unusual photography	☐ dramatic message	_____
3. ☐ catchy words	☐ good concept	☐ great music	_____
4. ☐ good actor	☐ humor	☐ unusual photography	_____
5. ☐ good actor	☐ humor	☐ effective photography	_____
6. ☐ clever message	☐ makes you think	☐ dramatic message	_____

ADVERTISING SURVEY

GROUP WORK. Complete the survey. Then discuss your answers to find out what kind of ads your classmates like.

MEMORABLE ADS

	PRODUCT	WHERE SEEN	SHORT DESCRIPTION
An ad for:			
fast food			
a soft drink			
a car			
An ad with:			
a famous athlete			
an actor or actress			
an animal			
catchy music			
An ad that's:			
simple			
funny			
dramatic			

A: My **favorite ad with catchy music** is the ad for Levi's jeans. Have you seen it?
B: Yeah, I know the one you mean. It's unusual. The one I like best is the one for Clairol shampoo. It's very funny.
A: Is that the one with the woman shampooing her hair in a taxi?
B: Yes, that's it.

UNIT 11 ADVERTISING

UNIT 12 MYSTERIES AND BELIEFS

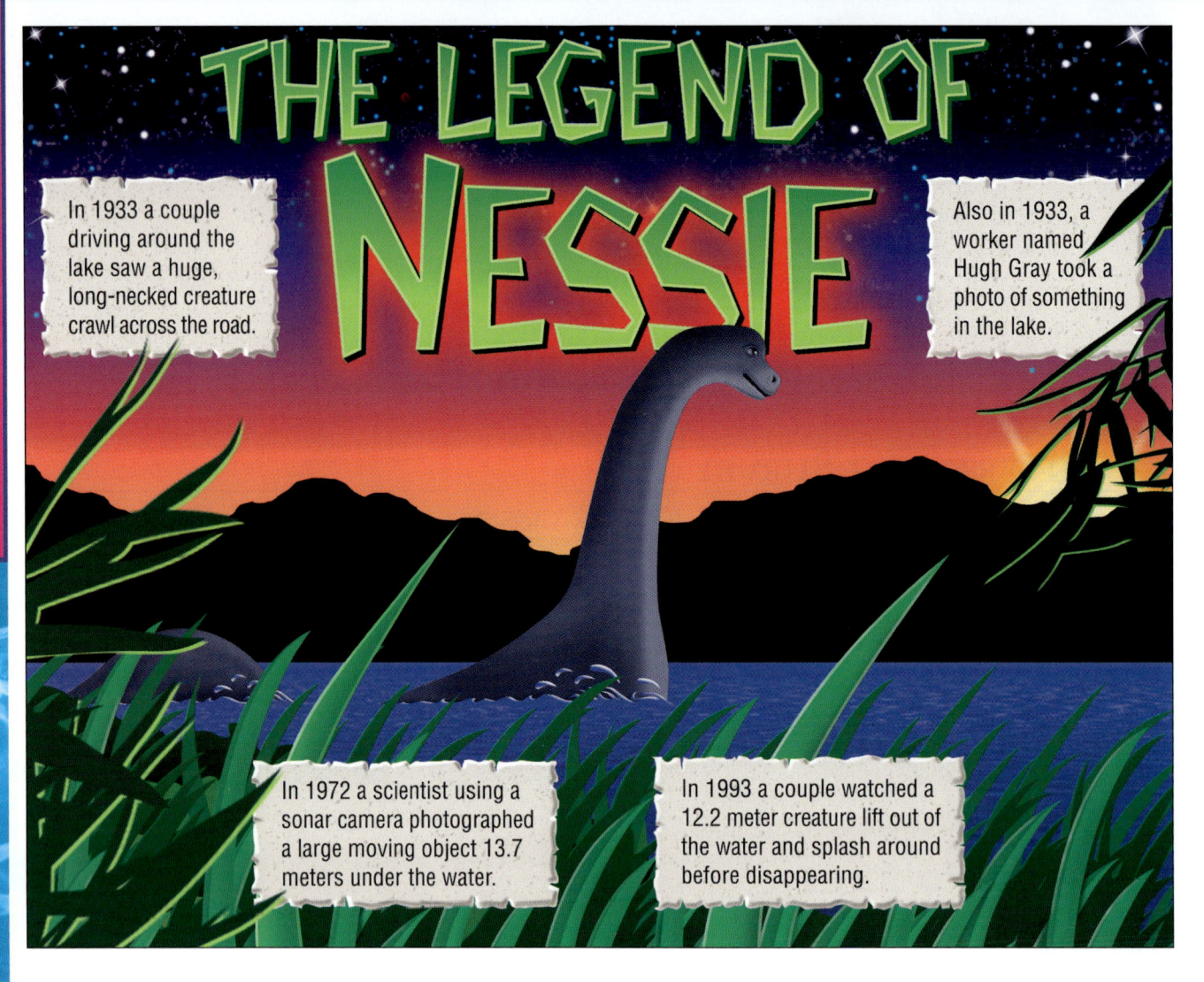

SPRINGBOARD

THE LEGEND OF NESSIE

In 1933 a couple driving around the lake saw a huge, long-necked creature crawl across the road.

Also in 1933, a worker named Hugh Gray took a photo of something in the lake.

In 1972 a scientist using a sonar camera photographed a large moving object 13.7 meters under the water.

In 1993 a couple watched a 12.2 meter creature lift out of the water and splash around before disappearing.

► NESSIE

A. Read the information above about a mysterious creature some people believe lives in Loch Ness, Scotland.

B. PAIR WORK. Do you believe in the Loch Ness monster? Discuss your ideas with a partner.

	Expressing Belief and Doubt
A: Do you believe there's really a monster in the lake? B: *I'm not sure. There could be.* Why not? A: *I suspect that* there's something there. Otherwise, how could you explain all those sightings?	I'm (not) sure there is... There could be... I suspect that... I doubt that... I'm not convinced that...

C. GROUP WORK. What other mysteries do you know about? Decide on and list three mysteries. Present your list to the class.

46 • UNIT 12 MYSTERIES AND BELIEFS

LISTENING

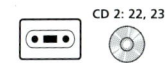

A. Listen to Mei Ling, Tim and Jackie discussing whether they believe in Nessie. Check (✔) *true believer*, *open-minded* or *skeptic* to describe each person.

B. Listen again. Write each person's *explanation* for Nessie.

	True Believer	Open-Minded	Skeptic	Explanation
1. Mei Ling				
2. Tim				
3. Jackie				

WORLD MYSTERIES

A. Read the four world mysteries and the explanations below.

Ghosts
Ghosts are spirits of dead people that died in their homes.

EXPLANATION:
The body dies, but the spirit lives on.

Nostradamus
Michel Nostradamus was a 16th century French astrologer and doctor. Some say he predicted the French Revolution, the Second World War and many other events.

EXPLANATION:
The stars can tell us many things. Nostradamus knew how to read them.

Yeti
The Yeti is a huge, fur-covered monster that lives in the Himalayas.

EXPLANATION:
The Yeti is a surviving caveman.

Near Death Experiences
People have near death experiences when they come close to dying. Many people have told stories of rising up, nearing a light, leaving their bodies and not wishing to return.

EXPLANATION:
These people had a look at the next life.

B. PAIR WORK. What do you think of the explanations? Discuss the explanations with your partner.

A: What do you think of the explanation for **Ghosts?** Do you agree?
B: *You bet!* I believe in ghosts. OR
  I'm not so sure. There might (not) be ghosts. OR
  No way! I don't believe in ghosts.
A: Yeah, I agree. OR Really? I...

Reacting to Explanations

You bet!	*I'm not so sure.*	*No way!*
Absolutely!	*I really can't say.*	*Impossible.*
Without a doubt!	*Who knows?*	*Are you kidding?*

UNIT 12 MYSTERIES AND BELIEFS

UNIT 12 MYSTERIES AND BELIEFS

PERSONAL BELIEFS

A. Look at things people believe in. Match each statement below with an object.

1. Tarot cards can be used for predicting your future.
2. Nature has forces that can influence your well-being.
3. The lines on your palms predict your future.
4. Special stones can help you find your inner wisdom.
5. This object of beads and feathers catches dreams.
6. This object lets you communicate with people that are not present.

B. PAIR WORK. Do you believe any of the things above? Describe your beliefs to your partner.

	Expressing Beliefs	
A: Do you think **cards can be used for predicting your future?**	open-minded | about curious	skeptical | about doubtful don't care
B: Well, I'm *skeptical about* it. It strikes me as pretty ridiculous. After all...	intrigued | by fascinated	
A: I guess I'm *open-minded about* it because...		not interested in

48 • UNIT 12 MYSTERIES AND BELIEFS

LISTENING

CD 2: 24, 25

A. Listen to people discussing their beliefs about the things below. Write one thing they believe about each topic.

B. Listen again. Where did each person get this belief from?

	BELIEF	SOURCE OF BELIEF
① plants		
② character		
③ the future		

BELIEVE IT OR NOT

A. PAIR WORK. Take turns asking your partner the **Belief Survey** questions. Keep track of your partner's beliefs and calculate his or her score.

BELIEF SURVEY

Agree Disagree

① UFOs probably exist.
② Ghosts are real.
③ Astrology is a science.
④ There are people who can predict the future.
⑤ Some people can read other people's minds.
⑥ After people die they come back in another form.
⑦ It's possible to communicate by thought to other people.
⑧ Aliens are living on earth disguised as humans.

Scoring:
True Believer —you agree with more than six
Open-minded —you agree with four to six
Skeptic —you disagree with five or more

	Responding
A: Do you believe **UFOs exist**? B: *Definitely not*. For me there's no proof of that.	*Definitely.* *There's lots of proof for that.* *It's very likely that it's true.* *It very well could be.* *Definitely not.* *It's not* | *possible.* | *scientific.* *There's no proof of that.*

B. GROUP WORK. Join another pair and report your belief scores. Then report the group's scores to the class.

UNIT 12 MYSTERIES AND BELIEFS • 49

Project File

SPRINGBOARD

Each project in the **Springboard Project File** has you:

▶ **PLAN** an activity that you will do inside or outside of class.

▶ **DO** the activity and make something that you can show others.

▶ **SHARE** the finished product of your activity with other students.

50 • PROJECT FILE

PROJECT **SPENDING DIARY**

UNIT 1

Where does your money go? Make a collage that shows how you spend your money.

🔧 Tool Box

🚩 Plan

Make a chart like the one below to keep track of how you spend your money.

Date	Item	Place Bought	Price
April 25	train ticket	station	$5.15
April 25	cup of coffee	Doug's Donuts	$1.95

🚩 Do

A. Write down every purchase you make for five days and enter it in your chart.

B. Organize the information in a collage. Sketch or paste items on your collage.

🚩 Share

A. Display all collages in class.

B. Where do you and your classmates spend most of your money? Compare your collage with your classmates'.

APRIL 25
station $5.15
Doug's Donuts $1.95

APRIL 26
McDonald's $4.29
7-11 .75¢

APRIL 27
Sun Theaters $8.50
Sun Theaters $3.50
station $3.00

UNIT 1 SPENDING DIARY • 51

UNIT 2

PROJECT STRESS WHEEL

Create a stress wheel to see if your life is in balance.

🔧 TOOL BOX

▶ PLAN

A. Read the areas that are often part of people's lives in the chart below.

____ emotions	____ relaxation	____ friends	____ work
____ education	____ time alone	____ family	____ health

B. Write a number from 1 (a little) to 5 (a lot) to indicate how much time you think you spend on each area.

▶ DO

A. Draw a stress wheel like the one on the right. Include all the areas you ranked above.

B. Write the numbers for each area from the chart above on the wheel. Then connect the numbers to find out where your life is out of balance. (Stressful areas will stick in or out from your circle.)

C. Connect the dots.

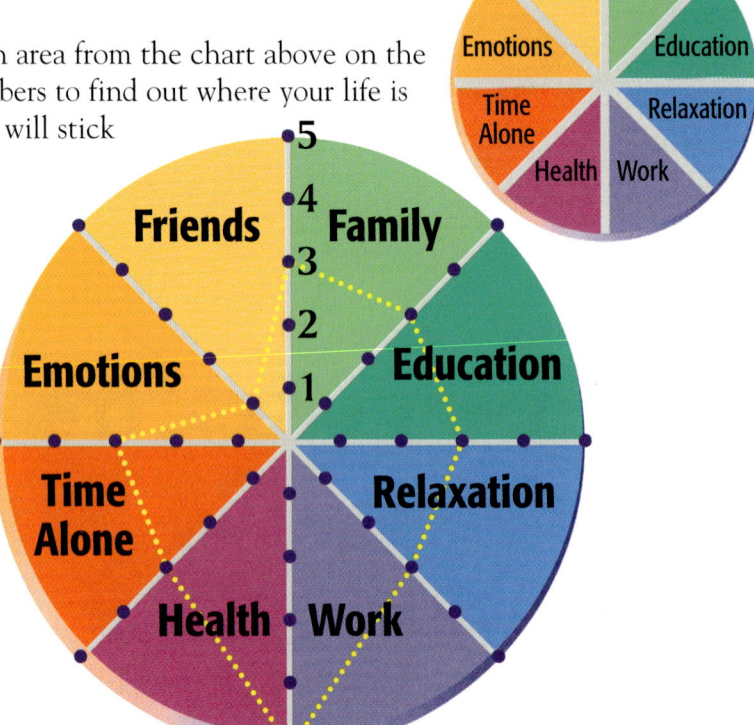

▶ SHARE

Compare stress wheels with your classmates'. Comment on the statement "Wheels need to be round to move along smoothly."

52 • UNIT 2 STRESS WHEEL

PROJECT RULES OF FRIENDSHIP

UNIT 3

What rules should friends follow with each other? Present your own five "Rules of Friendship."

🔧 TOOL BOX

▶ PLAN

Write five rules that are important to you in a friendship in the chart. Use language from the language box on page 10 to write your sentences.

RULES OF FRIENDSHIP

1. Friends need to have a similar sense of humor.

▶ DO

Make a sign or poster of your five "Rules of Friendship." Use your imagination to illustrate your rules.

▶ SHARE

Display your rules in class. Do you agree with your classmates' rules?

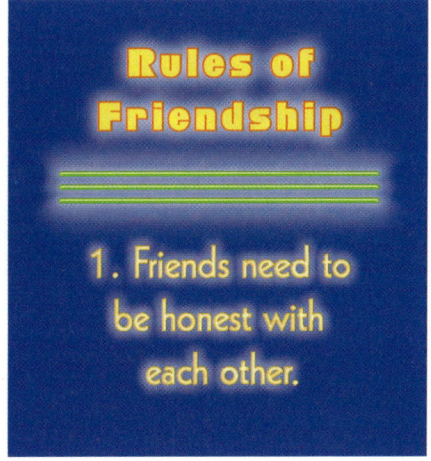

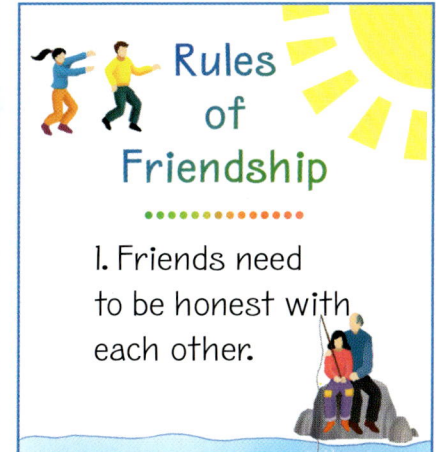

Rules of Friendship

1. Friends need to be honest with each other.

Rules of Friendship

1. Friends need to be honest with each other.

Rules of Friendship

1. Friends need to be honest with each other.

UNIT 3 RULES OF FRIENDSHIP • 53

UNIT 4 PROJECT AMAZING ACHIEVEMENT

Design a poster for an amazing achievement to present to the class.

🔧 TOOL BOX

▶ PLAN

Choose an amazing achievement to present to the class. Make a list of places to look for information about the achievement.

▶ DO

A. Collect as much information as you can about the achievement.
B. Choose the most important information to include in your poster. Use the model below.

Born: 9/6/75   Gold Medal: World Judo Championships   Ryoko Tamura "Yawara-chan"   Home: Fukuoka, Japan   Nickname: Yawara-chan

C. Design a poster of the amazing achievement.

▶ SHARE

Present your poster and explain the achievement to the class.

Name: Ryoko Tamura
Born: 9/6/75
Nickname: Yawara-chan

Achievement: Gold Medal World Judo Championships
October 12, 1997
Paris, France

54 • UNIT 4 AMAZING ACHIEVEMENT

PROJECT **EXOTIC GETAWAY**

UNIT 5

Compare package tours for an exotic getaway.

TOOL BOX

▶ PLAN

A. Choose an exotic getaway for which you would like to compare package tours.

B. Make a list of three places where you can collect travel brochures about your getaway.

1. _____ 2. _____ 3. _____

▶ DO

A. Record the information for two tours in a chart like the one below.

	Tour company	Hotel name	Hotel rating	Highlights	Length of trip	Total cost
Package 1						
Package 2						

B. Present your two plans in a poster.

▶ SHARE

Display and compare your travel plans. Have your classmates choose the best one.

Australian Getaways

Australian Pacific Tours
two-week getaway

★★★★★ The Reef Hotel Casino
Great Barrier Reef cruise
seaplane trips
scuba diving
A$2,700.00

VIP Tours
two-week getaway

▸ Ayers Rock Resort ★★★
▸ Uluru (Ayers Rock)
▸ gourmet bush barbecue
▸ 4WD tour
A$2,500.00

UNIT 5 EXOTIC GETAWAY • 55

UNIT 6 PROJECT ANIMAL MIRROR

People attribute human qualities to animals. Tell which animals reflect your personal qualities.

🔧 TOOL BOX

▶ PLAN

List as many of your personal qualities as you can. Then write an animal that reflects each quality.

Personal Qualities	Animals
e.g. clever	fox
shy	mouse

▶ DO

A. Collect pictures from newspapers and magazines or make sketches for the animals in your chart.
B. Arrange the animals in an interesting display and write the personal quality they represent.

▶ SHARE

A. Display all collages in class with blank sheets of paper next to them.
B. Write comments and guess the makers of the collages.

CLEVER   HARD-WORKING   ?   FAST   STRONG

56 • UNIT 6 ANIMAL MIRROR

PROJECT SONG CONTEST

UNIT 7

Enter your favorite song in English about partners in the song contest.

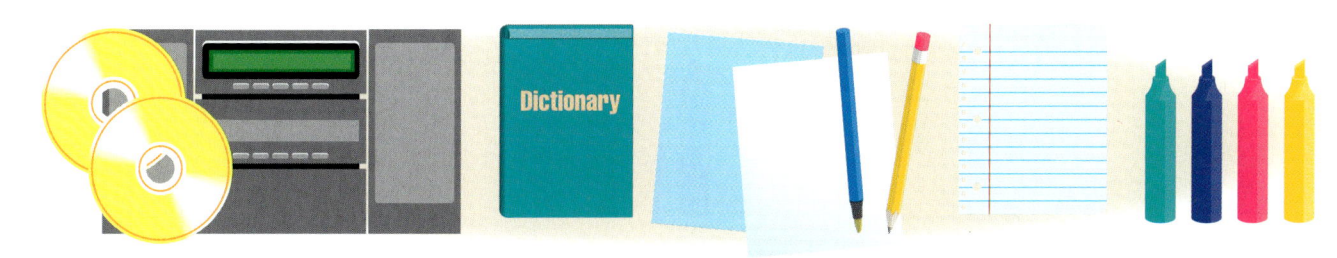

🔧 TOOL BOX

▶ PLAN

A. Select a favorite song about partners. Song title: _____

B. Make a list of possible sources where you can get the song lyrics. For example, CD liner notes.

1. _____   2. _____   3. _____

▶ DO

A. Find the song lyrics and arrange them in an interesting way on a sheet of paper.

B. Prepare a short glossary for the words you do not know. Use the model below.

▶ SHARE

A. Make copies for all your classmates.

B. Play a recording of your song in class and explain any new words and phrases.

C. Vote for your favorite song.

I Got You Babe

They say our love won't pay the rent,*

Before it's earned,* our money's always spent.*

I guess that's so,

*Glossary

rent (n.) - the money you pay for the use of something that you do not own (e.g. a house or apartment)

earn (v.) - get money by working

spend (v.) - pay money for something

UNIT 7 SONG CONTEST • 57

UNIT 8 PROJECT: T-SHIRT DESIGN

Design an original T-shirt.

🔧 TOOL BOX

▶ PLAN

A. Choose an organization to make a T-shirt for. For example, a club or music group.

B. Decide on the image and colors you will use and complete the chart.

Organization	Image	Colors

▶ DO

Draw your T-shirt on a poster. Write its best design qualities on the poster.

▶ SHARE

Display your T-shirt poster with your classmates'. Which ones are the most interesting? Which ones do you like the best?

BOLD COLORS **COOL!**

UNIQUE DESIGN **COMFORTABLE TO WEAR**

PIKE'S PEAK SKI CLUB

58 • UNIT 8 T-SHIRT DESIGN

PROJECT MY THEME PARK

UNIT 9

Plan a theme park for your neighborhood.

🔧 TOOL BOX

▶ PLAN

A. Choose a theme and a name for your park. For example, a dinosaur park or an ocean park.

Theme _____ Park Name _____

B. Think of a ride, a tour and a restaurant for your park.

	Ride	Tour	Restaurant
Name	e.g. Virtual Racer	Inside Computers	Cyber Cafe

▶ DO

Create a map for your park with ride, tour and restaurant images.

▶ SHARE

Display your map with your classmates'. Share your reactions to the posters.

UNIT 9 MY THEME PARK • 59

UNIT 10

PROJECT VALUES SURVEY

Create a survey to find out your classmates' values.

🔧 TOOL BOX

▶ PLAN

Write ten values questions about values such as generosity, self-sacrifice, modesty, loyalty, perseverance, ambition and honesty.

Category	Question
Ambition	Do you hope to be a company president someday?
Perseverance	Have you ever studied all night long?
Loyalty	Would you automatically change jobs for more money?

▶ DO

A. Design a values survey with your ten questions.

B. Make copies and survey ten friends or classmates.

C. Compile the information from the survey in an interesting way.

▶ SHARE

Display the results of your survey. Discuss them in small groups.

Values Survey — Yes / No

1. Do you hope to be a company president someday?
2. Have you ever studied all night long?
3. Would you automatically change jobs for money?

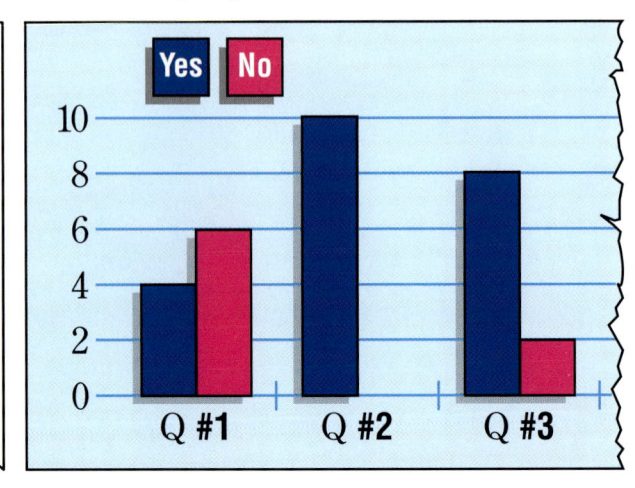

- UNIT 10 VALUES SURVEY

PROJECT BEST AD

UNIT 11

Make a poster of your favorite magazine or newspaper advertisements and tell why you think they are effective.

🔧 TOOL BOX

▶ PLAN

List three magazines or newspapers where you can find great ads.

1. _____   2. _____   3. _____

▶ DO

A. Collect three ads of different products from magazines or newspapers.

B. Write why you think these advertisements are effective in the chart below.

	Ad 1	Ad 2	Ad 3
Why it is effective			

C. Attach your three advertisements to a poster. Below each advertisement write expressions describing why you think the advertisement is effective.

▶ SHARE

A. Present and explain your ads.
B. Vote for the best ad.

Ad for "Tasty Snacks"
*uses good photography
*is eye-catching
*looks dramatic

UNIT 11 BEST AD • 61

UNIT 12

PROJECT LUCKY FOR ME

What are some of the lucky things in your life? Present them to the class.

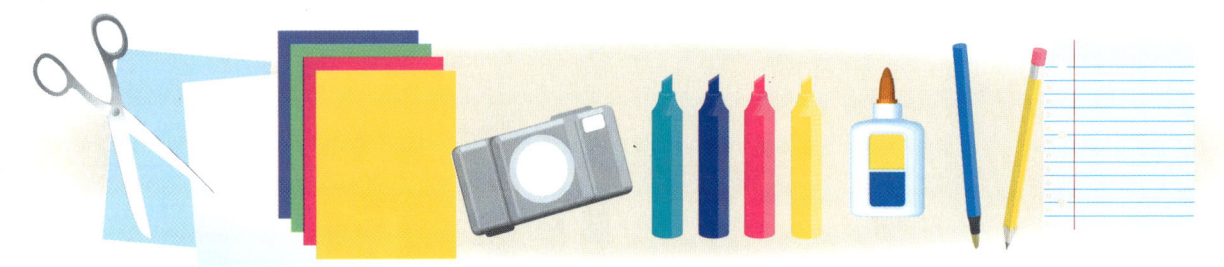

🔧 TOOL BOX

▶ PLAN

Think of the lucky things in your life. Write at least six things in a chart like the one below.

Lucky For Me

day _Monday_	number _____	charm _____	symbol _____
words _Good luck_	gesture _____	clothes _____	habits _____
animal _____	plant _____	food _____	other _____

▶ DO

Collect the things on your list, or sketches or photos of them.

▶ SHARE

A. Arrange your lucky things on a poster board or desktop.

B. Present your lucky things in small groups.

62 • UNIT 12: LUCKY FOR ME

Glossary

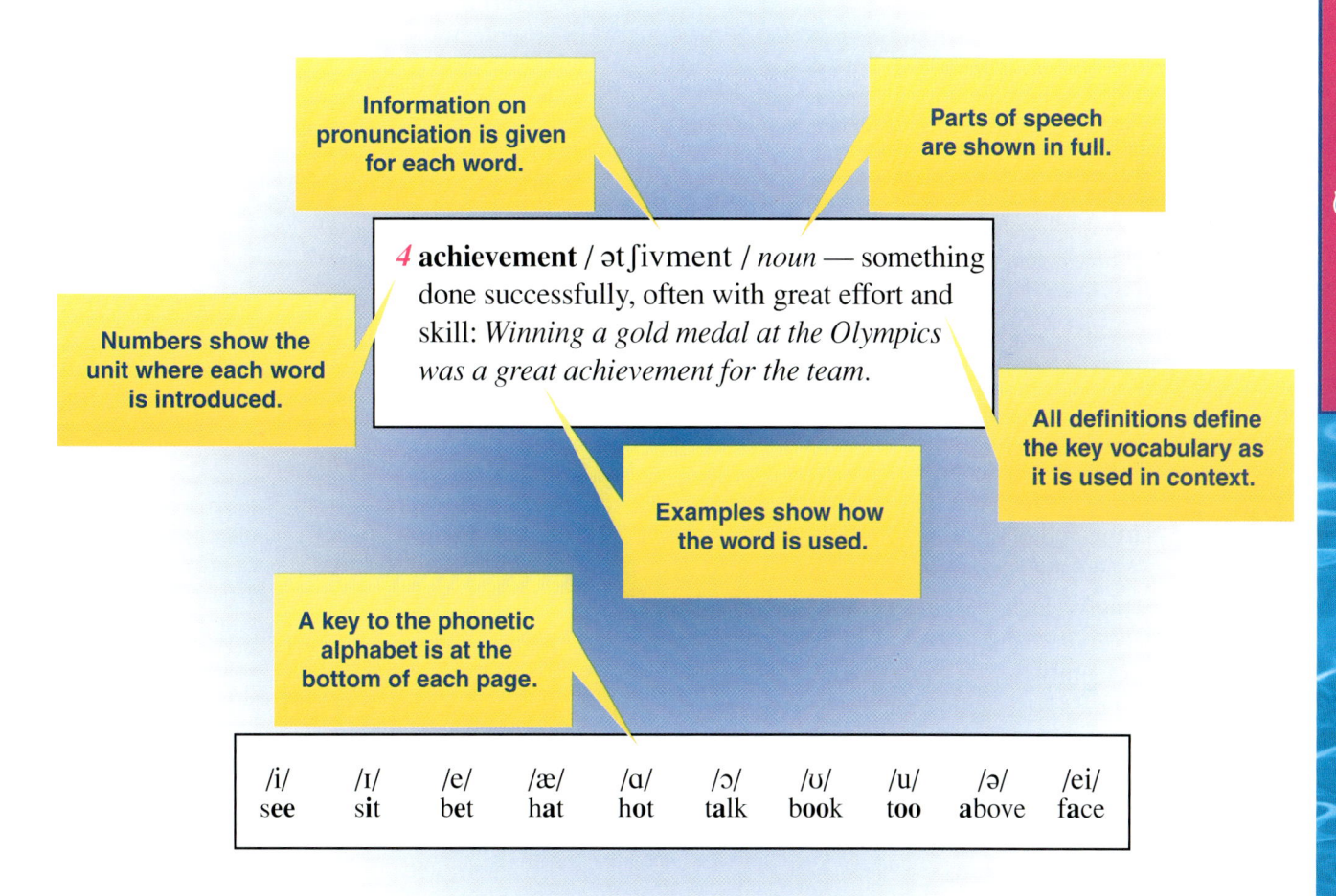

Information on pronunciation is given for each word.

Parts of speech are shown in full.

Numbers show the unit where each word is introduced.

4 **achievement** / ətʃivment / *noun* — something done successfully, often with great effort and skill: *Winning a gold medal at the Olympics was a great achievement for the team.*

All definitions define the key vocabulary as it is used in context.

Examples show how the word is used.

A key to the phonetic alphabet is at the bottom of each page.

/i/	/ɪ/	/e/	/æ/	/ɑ/	/ɔ/	/ʊ/	/u/	/ə/	/ei/
see	sit	bet	hat	hot	talk	book	too	above	face

The *Springboard* Glossary defines key vocabulary from the units and gives examples of how the words are used.

Use the *Springboard* Glossary to:

▶ Learn the meanings of key vocabulary words from the book.
▶ See examples of how key vocabulary words are used in context.
▶ Learn how key vocabulary words are pronounced.

SPRINGBOARD GLOSSARY • 63

absolutely incredible • break a promise

4 **absolutely incredible** / æbsəlutli ɪnkredəbəl / *adjective* — hard to believe, completely amazing. ("Absolutely" is an intensifier that makes the adjective even stronger): *The dancer's performance was absolutely incredible.*

4 **achieve a goal** / ətʃiv ə goul / *verb phrase* — to succeed in reaching a target or aim; doing something that is the object of your efforts: *She hopes to achieve her personal goal of climbing Mount Everest someday.*

4 **achievement** / ətʃivmənt / *noun* — something done successfully, often with great effort and skill: *Winning a gold medal at the Olympics was a great achievement for the team.*

5 **action-packed** / ækʃən pækt / *adjective* — full of activity, excitement, and adventure; not dull: *We took an action-packed white water rafting trip.*

6 **adorable** / ədɔrəbəl / *adjective* — very attractive, delightful, charming: *What an adorable child!*

5 **adventuresome** / ədventʃərsəm / *adjective* — bold, daring, full of exciting experiences: *an adventuresome trip into the jungle.*

9 **alien** / eiliən / *noun* — someone from another planet: *aliens from outer space.*

10 **ambition** / æmbɪʃən / *noun* — a strong desire to achieve something, such as success or fame: *She has a great ambition to succeed in business.*

9 **ancient ruins** / einʃənt ruɪnz / *noun* (plural) — a very old building (or buildings) that has been severely damaged or nearly destroyed: *the ancient ruins of China.*

8 **anger** / æŋgər / *noun* — a strong negative feeling you have when you are not pleased with something: *I said it in a moment of anger and now I'm sorry.*

3 **annoy** / ənɔi / *verb* — to irritate or make someone a little angry: *It annoys me when you leave your clothes all over the floor.*

8 **appealing** / əpiliŋ / *adjective* — attractive, nice to look at: *an appealing smile.*

7 **approval** / əpruvəl / *noun* — showing or saying that something is good or right: *I can't agree to anything without my partner's approval.*

7 **arranged marriage** / əreindʒd mærɪdʒ / *noun* — a marriage in which the parents choose the person their son or daughter will marry.

7 **as far as I'm concerned** / æz fɑr æz aim kənsərnd / *adverbial phrase* — so far as the matter is important to me or affects me (often used for giving opinions): *As far as I'm concerned, you can do what you like.*

12 **astrology** / əstrɑlədʒi / *noun* — the study of the positions and movements of the stars and planets in the belief that they have an effect on human affairs and behavior: *Do you believe that astrology has an effect on our lives?*

11 **athlete** / æθlit / *noun* — someone who has the strength and skill to perform well at sports: *He is a natural athlete.*

6 **(be) banned** / bænd / *verb, past participle* — officially forbidden or stopped: *Smoking is banned in many subway stations.*

12 **bead** / bid / *noun* — a small piece of wood, glass, etc., with a hole through it, often put together with others on a string or wire and sometimes worn as a necklace: *a string of glass beads.*

1 **beeper** / bipər / *noun* — a small electronic machine that "beeps" (makes a sound) to tell you that someone wants you to call them (also called a **pager**).

3 **belief** / bɪlif / *noun* — a feeling that something is true or real: *her belief in UFOs.*

5 **binoculars** / bɪnɑkyələrz / *noun* (plural) — an instrument with lenses for both eyes, which helps you see distant objects: *I use binoculars at rock concerts.*

10 **bootleg copy** / butleg kɑpi / *noun* — a recording, document, etc., that has been copied and/or sold illegally: *a bootleg cassette, recorded illegally at a concert.*

10 **break a promise** / breik ə prɑmɪs / *verb phrase* — to fail to do something you said you would definitely do; to fail to keep a promise: *Dad promised to take us to Disneyland this year, but he broke his promise.*

/i/	/ɪ/	/e/	/æ/	/ɑ/	/ɔ/	/ʊ/	/u/	/ə/	/ei/
see	sit	bet	hat	hot	talk	book	too	above	face

64 • SPRINGBOARD GLOSSARY

bug spray • do a favor

5 **bug spray** / bəg sprei / *noun* — a liquid forced out of a container in tiny drops onto the skin to keep away bugs: *This bug spray works well against annoying mosquitoes.*

1 **button** / bətən / *noun* — a round piece of plastic or metal that has a design or a message printed on it and can be pinned to clothing, bags, etc.

5 **calm** / kɑm / *adjective* — quiet, relaxed, not excited: *We spent a calm, relaxing weekend fishing on the lake.*

7 **career goals** / kərɪr goulz / *noun* (plural) — what you hope to achieve in your job or profession: *Right now, my main career goals are to become a manager and to have job satisfaction.*

5 **carefree** / kerfri / *adjective* — without any worries: *a carefree vacation in the mountains.*

11 **catchy** / kætʃi / *adjective* — easy to remember: *a catchy tune / catchy lyrics.*

12 **caveman** / keivmæn / *noun* — a person who lives in a **cave** (a hollow place in the side of a hill, or underground), especially in prehistoric times: *Cavemen probably drew pictures on cave walls.*

5 **cellular phone (cell phone)** / selyələr foun / *noun* — a cordless telephone that you can carry around with you, that uses radio signals to make it work.

10 **charge (someone) for** / tʃɑrdʒ fɔr / *verb phrase* — to ask someone for an amount of money as a price: *I complained to the waiter that my meal tasted awful, so he didn't charge me for it.*

10 **cheat** / tʃit / *verb* — to act dishonestly or unfairly in order to gain an advantage: *She was asked to leave school after she was caught cheating on an exam.*

8 **clash** / klæʃ / *verb* — to look bad together or not match: *The color of the wallpaper clashes with the color of the carpet; they look awful together.*

8 **cobalt blue** / koubɔlt blu / *adjective, noun* — a bright deep blue color.

11 **concept** / kɑnsept / *noun* — a general idea, principle or plan that relates to something abstract: *The movie's concept was fascinating.*

5 **cosmetics** / kɑzmetɪks / *noun* (plural) — substances designed to make the face, hair, and skin more beautiful: *Face powder, skin cream, and lipstick are cosmetics.*

12 **creature** / kritʃər / *noun* — a living being, sometimes imaginary or very strange: *creatures from under the sea / creatures from other planets.*

6 **creepy** / kripi / *adjective* — causing nervousness; strange in a disturbing way: *That ghost story was really creepy.*

6 **cruel** / kruəl / *adjective* — causing pain and suffering: *I think it's cruel to keep animals in cages.*

5 **cuddle** / kədəl / *verb* — to hold close and lovingly in one's arms; to hug. *The children cuddled their stuffed animals.*

6 **cuddly** / kədli / *adjective* — pleasant to cuddle (hold close and lovingly in one's arms): *a cuddly toy.*

5 **dance your heart out** / dæns yʊr hɑrt aut / *verb phrase* — to dance energetically, with a lot of feeling: *She danced her heart out at the disco last night.*

4 **dangerous** / deindʒərəs / *adjective* — something that is unsafe and can hurt you: *Diving into shallow water is dangerous.*

4 **daring** / derɪŋ / *adjective* — brave, bold, adventurous: *Trying out such a difficult jump was a daring thing for that ice skater to do.*

8 **design** / dəzain / *noun* — an arrangement of lines, shapes, and figures as decoration; a pattern: *a floral/abstract design.*

12 **disguised (as)** / dɪsgaizd / *adjective* — made to look or sound different from normal: *The boy went to the party disguised as a ghost.*

6 **disgusting** / dɪsgəstɪŋ / *adjective* — causing a strong feeling that something is very unpleasant: *Look at those bugs in the food — it's disgusting!*

11 **distinctive** / dɪstɪŋktɪv / *adjective* — having qualities that make something or someone different from others: *a distinctive appearance/style/laugh.*

3 **do a favor** / du ə feivər / *verb phrase* — to do something to help someone or to be kind: *Could you do me a favor and carry these boxes upstairs?*

/ou/	/ai/	/au/	/ɔi/	/p/	/b/	/t/	/d/	/k/	/g/
h**o**me	f**i**ve	**ou**t	b**oy**	**p**en	**b**ad	**t**en	**d**og	**c**at	**g**ot

doubtful (about) • feel pressured (by)

12 **doubtful (about)** / daʊtfəl / *adjective* — feeling doubts, not sure or certain about something: *I feel doubtful about going.*

8 **drab** / dræb / *adjective* — dull, not interesting: *These drab colors make me feel depressed.*

3 **drop everything** / drɑp evriθɪŋ / *verb phrase* — to stop whatever you are doing so that you can do something else: *When he heard about his son's accident, he dropped everything and rushed home.*

6 **educational** / edʒəkeɪʃənəl / *adjective* — providing education or teaching new things: *A trip to the zoo is very educational.*

11 **effective** / ɪfektɪv / *adjective* — producing the effect or result you want; making a strong and positive impression: *an effective speech.*

1 **electronic appliance** / ɪlektrɑnɪk əplaɪəns / *noun* — a machine or piece of equipment, such as a calculator, computer, or radio, that uses microchips or transistors to make it work.

6 **entertainer** / entərteɪnər / *noun* — someone who provides entertainment or amusement, often with a performance or a show: *street/TV entertainers.*

1 **entertainment** / entərteɪnment / *noun* — things you enjoy doing or seeing in your free time, such as video games, movies, concerts, etc.: *I usually go to the movies for entertainment.*

2 **escape from reality** / ɪskeɪp frəm riæləti / *verb phrase* — to get away from your personal situation or the problems in your life: *Playing video games is how I escape from reality.*

7 **essential** / ɪsenʃəl / *adjective* — extremely important, absolutely necessary: *Is money essential to happiness?*

5 **exotic** / ɪgzɑtɪk / *adjective* — strange or interesting because it comes from another country: *exotic fruits.*

3 **expenses** / ɪkspensəz / *noun* (plural) — money that you spend on certain things: *When I travel, my biggest expenses are airfare, hotels, and meals.*

11 **eye-catching** / aɪ kætʃɪŋ / *adjective* — noticeable, unusual, and interesting, especially because something is pleasant to look at: *an eye-catching poster/tie.*

12 **fascinated (by)** / fæsɪneɪtɪd / *adjective* — extremely interested in, and possibly attracted to, something or someone: *I am fascinated by the idea of life after death.*

7 **family background** / fæməli bækgraʊnd / *noun* — your experiences, financial situation, social status, etc., that come from your family: *a middle-class family background.*

3 **fashion sense** / fæʃən sens / *noun* — an understanding of and ability to judge fashion and style, especially in clothing: *Keiko's fashion sense is excellent; she even looks stylish in jeans.*

1 **fashionable** / fæʃənəbəl / *adjective* — in a fashion or style that is currently popular: *fashionable clothes, a fashionable hairstyle.*

11 **fast-food chain** / fæst fud tʃeɪn / *noun* — a group of restaurants, owned by the same company, that sells inexpensive food that is cooked and eaten quickly, such as hamburgers and French fries: *McDonald's and Burger King are fast-food chains.*

5 **fast-paced** / fæst peɪst / *adjective* — moving very quickly, with lots of activity: *He enjoys fast-paced video games.*

6 **feared enemy** / fɪrd enəmi / *noun* — someone or something that hates and wants to harm you, and makes you afraid: *Cats are feared enemies of mice.*

4 **feat** / fit / *noun* — something very difficult or dangerous that you do or achieve, which shows skill and courage: *Climbing that mountain was an amazing feat.*

12 **feather** / feðər / *noun* — one of the light coverings that grows from a bird's skin; a feather has a stem in the center with fine strands growing out on either side.

3 **(be) fed up (with)** / fed əp / *adjective* — unhappy with or tired of something that you would like to change: *I'm fed up with rush hour traffic.*

7 **feel pressured (by)** / fil preʃərd / *verb phrase* — to feel that someone else is trying to make you behave in a certain way or achieve something: *She feels pressured by her family to go to college.*

/f/	/v/	/θ/	/ð/	/s/	/z/	/ʃ/	/ʒ/	/tʃ/
fall	van	thin	then	sun	zoo	she	vision	chin

financial situation • (be) in control

7 **financial situation** / fənænʃəl sɪtʃueiʃən / *noun* — a financial position, or how much money someone currently has and needs: *My financial situation will improve as soon as I get a job.*

7 **find the love of one's life** / faind ðə ləv əv wɔnz laif / *verb phrase* — to meet the one person you love (romantically) more than anyone you've ever met before: *Anne is so happy; she met the love of her life and she's going to marry him.*

7 **find the right person** / faind ðə rait pərsən / *verb phrase* — to find or meet someone who is a good match: *Jim would like to get married, but he hasn't found the right person yet.*

8 **fire engine red** / faiər endʒɪn red / *adjective, noun* — a bright red color.

10 **flea market** / fli mɑrkɪt / *noun* — an outdoor market that sells old and used items, usually at low prices: *I got these old tea cups at a flea market.*

5 **flippers** / flɪpərz / *noun* (plural) — a pair of flat rubber shoes worn on the feet, to help you swim more quickly.

5 **4-wheel drive** / fɔr wil draiv / *noun* — a system in which power is given to all four wheels of a car or other vehicle: *The 4-wheel drive in this car makes it great for mountain roads.*

4 **frightening** / fraitənɪŋ / *adjective* — something that makes you feel afraid: *a frightening horror movie.*

10 **generosity** / dʒenərɑsɪti / *noun* — the quality of being generous — ready to give freely to others: *Some people show great generosity in giving to the poor.*

5 **get a (great) tan** / get ə tæn / *verb phrase* — to darken the color of skin by lying in the sun: *I got a great tan after a week at the beach.*

5 **get away from it all** / get əwei frəm ɪt ɔl / *verb phrase* — to have a relaxing and enjoyable vacation and not think about problems at home: *Let's go to Hawaii and get away from it all.*

2 **get caught in traffic** / get kɔt ɪn træfɪk / *verb phrase* — to become stuck or almost unable to move because there are so many other vehicles on the road: *I got caught in traffic on my way home from work.*

12 **ghost** / goust / *noun* — the spirit of a dead person: *Do you believe in ghosts?*

2 **give a speech** / gɪv ə spitʃ / *verb phrase* — to make, or deliver, a formal talk to an audience: *The President gave a speech on TV last night.*

5 **globetrotter** / gloubtrɑtər / *noun* — Someone who travels in many countries throughout the world.

2 **go online** / gou ɑnlain / *verb phrase* — to use your personal computer to connect (by telephone lines) to the Internet or other computer services: *I like to go online to check my e-mail and to surf the Internet.*

8 **go well together** / gou wel təgeðər / *verb phrase* — to combine well with, to match: *The colors of her blouse and skirt go well together.*

11 **graphics** / græfɪks / *noun* (plural) — designs, drawings, or pictures, especially for commercial use: *Good graphics are very important in advertising.*

2 **have a massage** / hæv ə məsɑʒ / *verb phrase* — when someone presses and rubs your body (especially the muscles) with the hands in order to reduce pain or to relax you: *I had a massage yesterday, and today I feel great!*

2 **have an argument** / hæv ən ɑrgyument / *verb phrase* — to have a difference of opinion with someone: *My roommate and I had an argument because I was playing music when he wanted to sleep.*

5 **health items** / helθ aitəmz / *noun* (plural) — cosmetics and items you can buy in a drugstore without a prescription, e.g. eye drops, Band-Aids, toothpaste.

8 **hole** / houl / *noun* — an opening, space, or gap in something solid: *I've worn holes in my socks.*

10 **honesty** / ɑnɪsti / *noun* — the quality of being honest and truthful; not lying, cheating, or stealing: *Everyone admires her honesty.*

3 **(be) in control** / ɪn kəntroul / *prepositional phrase* — to have the power to make others do what you want: *The teacher should be in control of the class.*

/dʒ/	/h/	/m/	/n/	/ŋ/	/l/	/r/	/y/	/w/
just	how	mark	none	sing	leg	red	yes	wet

SPRINGBOARD GLOSSARY • 67

independence • mouse pad

7 **independence** / ɪndɪpendəns / *noun* — freedom; no control from others: *She would like to get married and raise a family someday, but right now she wants her independence.*

12 **influence** / ɪnfluəns / *verb* — to have an effect on someone or something: *Don't let him influence your decision.*

7 **insignificant** / ɪnsɪgnɪfɪkənt / *adjective* — of little or no value, use, meaning, or importance: *A partner's looks are insignificant compared to his character.*

12 **intrigued (by)** / ɪntrigd / *adjective* — very interested in something, especially because it is unusual or mysterious: *Scientists are intrigued by the possibility of life on other planets.*

4 **involve** / ɪnvɑlv / *verb* — to include or have something as a part: *The job involves using a computer.*

4 **just plain dumb** / dʒəst pleɪn dəm / *adjective phrase* (informal) — clearly stupid or foolish: *Going swimming in a thunderstorm is just plain dumb.*

3 **keep a secret** / kip ə sikrɪt / *verb phrase* — to know something that only a few people know and not tell anyone else: *I never tell Steve anything private because he can't keep a secret.*

8 **kelly green** / keli grin / *adjective, noun* — a bright deep green color, often associated with Ireland

1 **key ring** / ki rɪŋ / *noun* — a metal or plastic ring to hold your keys, often with a piece of plastic attached with a design or logo on it: *That's a cool key ring.*

5 **laid-back** / leɪd bæk / *adjective* (informal) — relaxed and calm, not worried, easygoing: *a laid-back attitude/atmosphere.*

9 **landscape** / lændskeɪp / *noun* — everything you can see in an area of land: *a mountainous landscape.*

1 **latest** / leɪtəst / *adjective* — newest, most recent: *the latest style in shoes.*

8 **lavender** / lævendər / *adjective, noun* — a pale purple color.

8 **lemon yellow** / lemən yelou / *adjective, noun* — a bright yellow color, similar to the color of a lemon.

10 **let (someone) in for free** / let ɪn fɔr fri / *verb phrase* — to allow someone to go into a place or event without paying, even though they would normally pay: *The concert was half over when I arrived, so they let me in for free.*

10 **lie** / laɪ / *verb* — to say something that you know is not true; to tell a lie: *He lies about his age.*

8 **lime green** / laɪm grin / *adjective, noun* — a yellowish-green color, similar to the color of a lime.

10 **listen in on** / lɪsən ɪn ɑn / *verb* — to hear something that you are not supposed to be listening to; to listen to a conversation secretly: *She loves to listen in on other people's conversations.*

11 **logo** / lougou / *noun* — a printed symbol designed for and used by a company or organization as its special sign, for example, in advertising: *The logo for Apple Computer is a multicolored apple with a bite taken out.*

7 **love marriage** / lʌv mærɪdʒ / *noun* — a marriage of two people who are in love with each other; not an arranged marriage.

10 **loyalty** / lɔɪəlti / *noun* — the quality of being faithful and loyal: *loyalty to one's country.*

8 **magenta** / mədʒentə / *adjective, noun* — a color between purple and red.

2 **make a fool of myself** / meɪk ə ful əv maɪself / *verb phrase* — to do something that makes you look silly or laughable: *I wore two different color socks to school and made a fool of myself.*

5 **mask** / mæsk / *noun* — a covering for part of the face, used for protection.

9 **milk a cow** / mɪlk ə kaʊ / *verb phrase* — to take or squeeze milk from a cow: *Cows must be milked twice a day.*

10 **modesty** / mɑdɪsti / *noun* — the quality of being modest; not having too high an opinion about oneself or boasting about one's abilities, qualities, etc.: *He is modest about his achievements.*

1 **mouse pad** / maʊs pæd / *noun* — a small rubber sheet that you use on a table or desk for a **mouse** — a small object attached to a computer, which you hold in your hand and move around in order to give the computer commands.

/i/	/ɪ/	/e/	/æ/	/ɑ/	/ɔ/	/ʊ/	/u/	/ə/	/eɪ/
see	sit	bet	hat	hot	talk	book	too	above	face

SPRINGBOARD GLOSSARY

multimedia • racquet or racket

9 **multimedia** / məltimidiə / *adjective* — involving different methods of communication, such as video, graphics, sound, music, words, etc., especially for entertainment: *a multimedia event, including music, dance, video, and a laser show.*

8 **mustard** / məstərd / *adjective, noun* — a fairly dark yellow color, like the color of mustard (a hot-tasting yellow paste, eaten with food, especially meats): *a mustard (yellow) sweater.*

6 **natural** / nætʃərəl / *adjective* — normal or usual, part of the character of a living thing: *It's natural for some animals to eat smaller animals.*

5 **natural wonder** / nætʃərəl wəndər / *noun* — a place or thing existing in or caused by nature (not made by people) that causes a feeling of surprise or delight: *The Grand Canyon is a natural wonder.*

8 **not very original** / nɑt veri ərɪdʒənəl / *adjective* — not fresh or new, not creative: *That car looks like all the others; the design is not very original.*

1 **odds and ends** / ɑdz ən enz / *noun phrase* — different small things of little value: *I keep a lot of odds and ends in my desk drawer.*

12 **open-minded** / oupən maindɪd / *adjective* — willing to listen to and consider new ideas or opinions, not prejudiced: *I wish my parents were more open-minded about my friends.*

3 **opinion** / əpɪnyən / *noun* — your ideas or judgment about something or someone: *What's your opinion of rap music?*

6 **organ donor** / ɔrgən dounər / *noun* — someone who gives a part of the body (e.g., heart, kidney), sometimes at death, to help sick people: *The heart transplant will take place when an organ donor is found.*

4 **oyster** / ɔɪstər / *noun* — a small sea animal with a rough, grayish shell. Some types of oysters produce meat that can be eaten, and some produce pearls.

12 **palm** / pɑm / *noun* — the inner surface of the hand between the wrist and fingers: *Fortune tellers say they can read your palm and tell what will happen to you in the future.*

8 **passion** / pæʃən / *noun* — a strong feeling (either positive or negative), for example, of love, hate, or anger: *She argued with great passion.*

8 **peace** / pis / *noun* — a state of calm or quiet: *I enjoy the peace of a summer evening.*

8 **periwinkle blue** / periwɪŋkəl blu / *adjective, noun* — a light purplish-blue color.

10 **perseverance** / pərsəvirəns / *noun* — continued steady effort to achieve an aim or goal: *After months of disappointment, her perseverance was finally rewarded.*

5 **pet** / pet / *verb* — to stroke, or move your hands gently over an animal, etc.: *My dog loves it when I pet him.*

1 **platform sneakers** / plætfɔrm snikərz / *noun* (plural) — sneakers with very thick rubber soles: *How can she play sports in those platform sneakers?*

6 **playful** / pleifəl / *adjective* — full of fun, fond of playing: *playful kittens/children.*

1 **pocket money** / pɑkɪt məni / *noun* — money you spend on small things: *She spends all her pocket money on video games.*

12 **predict the future** / prɪdɪkt ðə fyutʃər / *verb phrase* — to say in advance what will happen at a later time: *If I could predict the future, I'd be rich!*

4 **pretty amazing** / prɪti əmeizɪŋ / *adjective* — fairly surprising. (Here, "pretty" means "rather" or "fairly," but not "attractive"): *The magician's tricks were pretty amazing.*

4 **pretty pointless** / prɪti pɔintlɪs / *adjective* — with little or no purpose; fairly useless: *It's pretty pointless to memorize grammar rules without understanding them.*

12 **proof** / pruf / *noun* — information that shows, or helps to show, that something is true or is a fact: *Is there proof of life on other planets?*

6 **protector** / prətektər / *noun* — someone who protects, guards, or keeps others safe from harm: *My dog is a great protector.*

1 **proverb** / prɑvərb / *noun* — a short sentence that is widely known and often gives advice about life: *"Variety is the spice of life" is an old proverb.*

4 **racquet or racket** / rækɪt / *noun* — a light, stringed bat used for hitting the ball in tennis, badminton, squash, and other games.

/ou/	/ai/	/au/	/ɔi/	/p/	/b/	/t/	/d/	/k/	/g/
home	five	out	boy	pen	bad	ten	dog	cat	got

SPRINGBOARD GLOSSARY

raise a family • skeptical

7 **raise a family** / reiz ə fæməli / *verb phrase* — to have children and care for them until they grow up: *They have raised ten children.*

10 **read someone's mail** / rid səmwənz meil / *verb phrase* — to read another person's letters, or other items received in the mail, when you aren't supposed to: *Be careful — she might read your mail when you're not looking.*

12 **read someone's mind** / rid səmwənz maind / *verb phrase* — to know what someone else is thinking: *How did you know what I was going to say? Can you read my mind?*

4 **really something** / riəli səmθɪŋ / *pronoun* — special, impressive, or unusual; having a strong favorable effect: *That tennis match was really something.*

3 **refuse (to)** / rɪfyuz / *verb phrase* — to say 'no' when someone asks you to do something: *His parents refused to give him any more money.*

2 **relax** / rɪlæks / *verb* — to become less stiff or tight (relax the muscles) or to reduce stress and become calmer: *I went on vacation in Hawaii to relax.*

2 **rent** / rent / *verb* — to pay money for the use of something that you do not own: *The video store was having a special, so I rented four videos for the weekend.*

3 **respond** / rɪspɔnd / *verb* — to react or act in answer to someone else's actions or words: *I tried to be friendly, but she didn't respond / she responded with silence.*

4 **risky** / rɪski / *adjective* — something that is full of danger and has the possibility of injury or loss: *Riding a motorcycle without a helmet is risky.*

4 **rough** / rʌf / *adjective* — not calm or gentle: *Rugby is a rough sport.*

2 **rush hour** / rʌʃ auər / *noun* — the time when a lot of people are coming from or going to work, a lot of cars are on the road, and subways and buses are crowded: *Traffic is heavy during rush hour.*

8 **sadness** / sædnɪs / *noun* — the feeling of being sad or unhappy: *He was filled with sadness after his wife's death.*

9 **satellite** / sætəlait / *noun* — an electronic device that is sent into space and moves around a planet: *a weather/communications satellite.*

9 **save it for next time** / seiv ɪt fɔr nekst taim / *verb phrase* — an expression used ironically to mean that you are unenthusiastic about something and prefer not to do it: *The kids wanted me to take them on the roller coaster at the theme park, but I told them to save it for next time.*

6 **scary** / skeri / *adjective* — causing fear: *That lightning storm was scary.*

6 **scientific participant** / saiəntifɪk pɑrtɪsəpənt / *noun* — someone who participates, or takes part, in scientific experiments: *Some people are willing to be scientific participants in studies to find cures for diseases.*

1 **selection** / sɪlekʃən / *noun* — a collection, choice, or variety of things — a great selection means a group of things with a lot of variety or different choices: *This store has a great selection of jeans.*

10 **self-sacrifice** / self sækrɪfais / *noun* — giving up needs, wishes, and things you want for yourself to help others: *His work with refugees involved a lot of self-sacrifice.*

3 **share** / ʃer / *verb* — to divide something into parts, between two or more people: *If you go Dutch at a restaurant, you share expenses, so each person pays for their own meal.*

12 **sighting** / saitɪŋ / *noun* — an occasion of something or someone being seen: *sightings of a new star.*

7 **silly** / sɪli / *adjective* — stupid, foolish: *Please don't call me 'sweetie pie' in front of other people; it sounds silly.*

5 **sip a drink** / sɪp ə drɪŋk / *verb phrase* — to drink something slowly, a little bit at a time: *Let's sit by the pool and sip our drinks.*

11 **simple** / sɪmpəl / *adjective* — plain and uncomplicated in form or design; without much decoration: *a simple black dress.*

12 **skeptic** / skeptɪk / *noun* — someone who doubts or does not believe that something is true because there is no definite proof: *When it comes to astrology, I'm a skeptic.*

12 **skeptical (about)** / skeptɪkəl / *adjective* — doubtful, unwilling to believe that something is true: *I'm skeptical about his chances of winning, no matter what people say.*

/f/	/v/	/θ/	/ð/	/s/	/z/	/ʃ/	/ʒ/	/tʃ/
fall	van	thin	then	sun	zoo	she	vision	chin

sleeping bag • (be) tied down

5 **sleeping bag** / slipɪŋ bæg / *noun* — a warm lined bag that you sleep in when you go camping.

6 **smart** / smɑrt / *adjective* — intelligent; having a good, quick brain: *a smart student.*

5 **snorkel** / snɔrkəl / *noun* — a tube that allows you to breathe air while swimming underwater.

2 **solution** / səluʃən / *noun* — a way of dealing with a difficulty or solving a problem: *My favorite solution for stress is having a cup of herbal tea.*

3 **sore** / sɔr / *adjective* — tender and painful because of too much exercise or too much use: *sore muscles, sore feet.*

9 **souvenir** / suvənir / *noun* — a thing that you buy, take, or receive as a gift, and keep to remind you of a person, place or event: *a souvenir program of the concert.*

6 **space traveler** / speis trævələr / *noun* — someone who travels outside the earth's atmosphere to where the other planets and stars are: *Do you think space travelers will visit Mars someday?*

8 **spirituality** / spɪrɪtʃuæləti / *noun* — the state of being concerned with matters of the human spirit or soul, rather than physical things: *Her spirituality helps her with any troubles in life.*

2 **stress** / stres / *noun* — a feeling of worry, pressure, or tension because of problems in one's life: *Her job is very difficult and causes her a lot of stress.*

8 **strike you as** / straik yu æz / *verb phrase* — to give someone a particular impression: *He strikes me as a very intelligent person.*

8 **striking** / straikɪŋ / *adjective* — attracting attention because it is unusual or interesting: *a striking color/design.*

9 **submarine** / səbmərin / *noun* — a ship that operates underwater.

6 **suffering** / səfərɪŋ / *noun* — pain of the body or mind: *There is too much suffering in the world.*

5 **sunscreen** / sənskrin / *noun* — a cream or lotion that you put on your skin to protect it from the sun: *I always put on sunscreen at the beach so I won't get sunburned.*

12 **surviving** / sərvaivɪŋ / *adjective* — continuing to live or exist: *the last surviving member of the family.*

3 **take (someone) for granted** / teik fɔr græntəd / *verb phrase* — to be so familiar with someone that you no longer appreciate them: *After a few months of marriage, she started to take her husband for granted.*

2 **take a nap** / teik ə næp / *verb phrase* — to have a short sleep, especially during the day: *I like to take a nap for about 30 minutes in the afternoon.*

3 **talk behind someone's back** / tɔk bihaind səmwənz bæk / *verb phrase* — to say negative things about someone when that person is not present: *They're always talking about him behind his back.*

8 **tangerine** / tændʒərin / *adjective, noun* — an orange color, similar to the color of a tangerine.

12 **tarot cards** / tɑrou kɑrdz / *noun (plural)* — a set of special cards with pictures on them, used to predict people's futures: *Fortune tellers sometimes use tarot cards to predict someone's future.*

3 **taste (in music)** / teist / *noun* — personal likes and dislikes about music, art, literature, clothes, etc.: *He has strange taste in music / good taste in clothes.*

5 **tee off** / ti ɔf / *verb* — to hit a golf ball off a **tee** (a small piece of wood, plastic, etc., that holds the ball): *Be quiet! I'm teeing off and I don't want to miss the ball!*

7 **terms of endearment** / tərmz əv endirment / *noun (plural)* — names you call someone that show affection or love: *'Darling' and 'Honey' are terms of endearment.*

4 **thrilling** / θrɪlɪŋ / *adjective* — very exciting: *a thrilling ride at the amusement park.*

5 **(a) thrill a minute** / θrɪl ə mɪnɪt / *noun phrase (informal)* — continual excitement: *That ride at the amusement park was a thrill a minute.*

3 **ticked off** / tɪkt ɔf / *adjective (informal)* — irritated or angry. *I was really ticked off when you didn't show up for our date.*

7 **(be) tied down** / taid daun / *adjective* — restricted to certain conditions, or a place, or a person; not free: *Kim didn't like being tied down, so she broke up with her boyfriend.*

/dʒ/	/h/	/m/	/n/	/ŋ/	/l/	/r/	/y/	/w/
just	how	mark	none	sing	leg	red	yes	wet

GLOSSARY

tight with money • water bottle

3 **tight with money** / taıt wıθ məni / *adjective phrase* — not willing to spend much money: *Don't ask her to take a taxi; she'd rather walk because she's tight with money.*

3 **tightwad** / taıtwɑd / *noun* — someone who is stingy and hates to spend money: *He's a real tightwad.*

4 **totally ridiculous** / toutəli rıdıkyələs / *adjective* — so silly that it makes people laugh. ("Totally" is an intensifier that makes the adjective even stronger): *It's totally ridiculous to try to play tennis with a football!*

9 **tour** / tur / *verb* — to visit a number of places on one trip: *We toured Europe on our vacation.*

9 **traditional** / trədıʃənəl / *adjective* — according to the beliefs and customs passed from one generation to the next; established methods, practices, ceremonies, etc.: *She wears the traditional clothes of her country.*

9 **tropical** / trɑpıkəl / *adjective* — of the tropics: *a tropical climate; tropical forests/fish.*

12 **true believer** / tru bılivər / *noun* — someone who believes strongly in a faith, principle, set of ideas, etc. and is completely dedicated to the cause.

6 **trusted companion** / trəstıd kəmpænyən / *noun* — someone you can rely on, or trust, who spends a lot of time with you: *A seeing eye dog is the trusted companion of a blind person.*

8 **turquoise blue** / tərkoız blu / *adjective, noun* — a light-bluish color like the gemstone turquoise.

12 **UFO** / yuefou / *noun* (abbreviation) — unidentified flying object, a spaceship from another planet: *Many UFO reports turn out to be shooting stars or ordinary airplanes.*

6 **uncivilized** / ənsıvəlaızd / *adjective* — not acceptable according to your society's moral standards: *Many people believe using animals as scientific participants is uncivilized.*

6 **unfair** / ənfeər / *adjective* — not right, just, or fair: *Many students thought the school rules were unfair.*

9 **unforgettable** / ənfərgetəbəl / *adjective* — something that will stay in your memory forever: *an unforgettable moment.*

8 **unique** / yunik / *adjective* — unlike anything else, the only one of its kind: *a unique design/opportunity.*

6 **unnatural** / ənnætʃərəl / *adjective* — not natural; different from what is normal or expected: *Keeping a lion as a pet is unnatural.*

2 **unwind** / ənwaınd / *verb* — to relax and feel calmer, especially after a period of stress, tension, or exhausting work: *I like to go out dancing after work; it helps me unwind.*

8 **up-to-date** / əp tu deit / *adjective* — modern, fashionable: *He wears clothes that are right up-to-date.*

10 **values** / vælyuz / *noun* (plural) — moral standards of behavior; principles about what is right or wrong: *Young people often have different values from their parents.*

9 **value for money** / vælyu fɔr məni / *noun phrase* — the worth of something compared with the price you paid for it: *Disneyland is the park with the best value for money.*

1 **variety** / vəraıəti / *noun* — many different things: *There's a large variety of dishes on the menu.*

9 **vase** / veis / *noun* — a container made of glass, china, clay, etc., and used for holding flowers or as an ornament: *Put these flowers in a vase.*

1 **video game** / vıdiou geim / *noun* — an electronic game that you play on a computer or an electronic device. The player controls the images on the screen: *I like the Nintendo video games.*

10 **virtue** / vərtʃu / *noun* — a quality in someone's character that shows high moral standards; goodness: *Patience is a virtue.*

10 **wallet** / wɑlıt / *noun* — a folding case of leather, plastic etc., carried in a pocket or handbag and used to hold money and credit cards: *I don't keep much cash in my wallet.*

8 **wardrobe** / wɔrdroub / *noun* — a person's collection of clothes: *I want to buy a whole new wardrobe for summer.*

1 **water bottle** / wɑtər bɑtəl / *noun* — a bottle, usually made of plastic, for carrying water by people who are exercising, bicycling, hiking, etc.: *I always take a water bottle when I go running.*

/i/	/ı/	/e/	/æ/	/ɑ/	/ɔ/	/ʊ/	/u/	/ə/	/ei/
see	sit	bet	hat	hot	talk	book	too	above	face

72 • SPRINGBOARD GLOSSARY

water slide • wood carver

9 **water slide** / wɑtər slaɪd / *noun* — a smooth, slippery surface on an incline, with water coming down it, for people to slide downward into a pool of water, for fun and recreation.

12 **well-being** / wɛl biɪŋ / *noun* — the state of being healthy, happy, etc.: *Do you have a sense of well-being?*

12 **wisdom** / wɪzdəm / *noun* — good sense; the ability to make good judgments because of your experience and knowledge: *an old woman of great wisdom.*

9 **wood carver** / wʊd kɑrvər / *noun* — someone who forms objects of art by cutting away at wood: *That wood carver makes beautiful dolls.*

Unit 1 Money
beeper
button
electronic appliance
entertainment
fashionable
key ring
latest
mouse pad
odds and ends
platform sneakers
pocket money
proverb
selection
variety
video game
water bottle

Unit 2 Stress and Solutions
escape from reality
get caught in traffic
give a speech
go online
have a massage
have an argument
make a fool of myself
relax
rent
rush hour
solution
stress
take a nap
unwind

Unit 3 Friendship
annoy
belief
do a favor
drop everything
expenses
fashion sense
(be) fed up (with)
(be) in control
keep a secret
opinion
refuse (to)
respond
share
sore
take (someone) for granted
talk behind someone's back
taste (in music)
ticked off
tight with money
tightwad

Unit 4 Challenges
absolutely incredible
achieve a goal
achievement
dangerous
daring
feat
frightening
involve
just plain dumb
oyster
pretty amazing
pretty pointless
racquet or racket
really something
risky
rough
thrilling
totally ridiculous

Unit 5 Globetrotters
action-packed
adventuresome
binoculars
bug spray
calm
carefree
cellular phone
cosmetics
cuddle
dance your heart out
exotic
fast-paced
flippers
4-wheel drive
get a (great) tan
get away from it all
globetrotter
health items
laid-back
mask
natural wonder
pet
sip a drink
sleeping bag
snorkel
sunscreen
tee off
(a) thrill a minute

Unit 6 Animals
adorable
(be) banned
creepy
cruel
cuddly
disgusting
educational
entertainer
feared enemy
natural
organ donor
playful
protector

SPRINGBOARD GLOSSARY • 73

GLOSSARY

scary
scientific participant
smart
space traveler
suffering
trusted companion
uncivilized
unfair
unnatural

Unit 7 Partners
approval
arranged marriage
as far as I'm concerned
career goals
essential
family background
feel pressured (by)
financial situation
find the love of one's life
find the right person
independence
insignificant
love marriage
raise a family
silly
terms of endearment
(be) tied down

Unit 8 Color and Design
anger
appealing
clash
cobalt blue
design
drab
fire engine red
go well together
hole
kelly green
lavender
lemon yellow
lime green
magenta
mustard
not very original

passion
peace
periwinkle blue
sadness
spirituality
strike you as
striking
tangerine
turquoise blue
unique
up-to-date
wardrobe

Unit 9 Theme Parks
alien
ancient ruins
landscape
milk a cow
multimedia
satellite
save it for next time
souvenir
submarine
tour
traditional
tropical
unforgettable
value for money
vase
water slide
wood carver

Unit 10 Values
ambition
bootleg copy
break a promise
charge (someone) for
cheat
flea market
generosity
honesty
let (someone) in for free
lie
listen in on
loyalty
modesty

perseverance
read someone's mail
self-sacrifice
values
virtue
wallet

Unit 11 Advertising
athlete
catchy
concept
distinctive
effective
eye-catching
fast-food chain
graphics
logo
simple

Unit 12 Mysteries and Beliefs
astrology
bead
caveman
creature
disguised (as)
doubtful (about)
fascinated (by)
feather
ghost
influence
intrigued (by)
open-minded
palm
predict the future
proof
read someone's mind
sighting
skeptic
skeptical (about)
surviving
tarot cards
true believer
UFO
well-being
wisdom